A New Level — A New Consciousness

The Phenomena of Barack Obama

Volume 1

by

Wade Lewis (The Magic Man)

authorHOUSE®

AuthorHouse™
1663 Liberty Drive
Bloomington, IN 47403
www.authorhouse.com
Phone: 1-800-839-8640

First published by AuthorHouse 7/9/2009

ISBN: 978-1-4389-9507-6 (e)
ISBN: 978-1-4389-9505-2 (sc)
ISBN: 978-1-4389-9506-9 (hc)

Library of Congress Control Number: 2009905769

Printed in the United States of America
Bloomington, Indiana

This book is printed on acid-free paper.

Contents

Foreword

I am inspired and deeply motivated to write this book, because I deeply, intuitively, and prophetically feel that Barack Obama is destined to be our next president and that he is grounding a political dynamics and political energy that this country and the world have not seen in a long time. This is a divine political energy in which this nation and the world need to advance to a higher level of government and politics.

These high-level political and social learnings that I am transcribing in this book are some of the most advanced that I have ever grounded in my political writings; therefore, I am so thankful, gracious, deeply appreciative, and humbled to be able to mentally go into the political universe and receive these advanced political learnings, political philosophies, political wisdom, political knowledge, and these higher political levels, political consciousness and political awareness.

Even though I knew Barack had a high political intellect and an extraordinary political and social dynamics when I heard him speak on television at the democratic convention in 2004, the inspiration and motivation to write this book grounded when Oprah Winfrey publicly endorsed him in December of 2007. I was emotionally moved and thrilled to know that Oprah, like me, recognized this high-level political phenomenon and put her political judgment on the line by endorsing him and his timely and hopeful message of change. I was even more inspired that Oprah intuitively knew and passionately believed that Barack represented change and was a personification of great political changes to come. She fully understood, even before Barack became well-known, that he represented the ending and the beginning: the ending of traditional politics as usual and the beginning of a new, politically inspiring vision of how to govern this great nation.

My deepest hope is that everyone who reads this book will be inspired like Obama, Oprah Winfrey, myself, and the millions of Americans in this nation and that every American citizen will enthusiastically participate in our political system and unite under this great national and international umbrella of hope and "yes we can do better." I am so excited and overjoyed to be one of the political and social ambassadors of this new age of political and social enlightenment, an age of enlightenment that has already redefined politics in America.

The great political vision that Barack Obama has laid out for this nation is the beginning of and is rooted out of this great new age of political enlightenment . This age of political enlightenment is creating a nation that is destined to be better and to reach a higher level of leadership from the people and our nation's leaders.

May God bless every American citizen and give each of you the highest and greatest political, social, and personal vision that you can create, ground, and make a reality in this great nation, the United States of America.

Wade Lewis (The Magic Man)

Introduction

The 2008 presidential election will be one of the most politically dynamic, energetic, and politically consciousness-driven elections that we Americans and the world will have experienced and witnessed in recent history. Not in the last fifty to seventy years has the majority of Americans so desperately and deeply desired such a massive, expansive, and drastic change in American government, politics, and national political leadership.

During every presidential election, there are always those citizens or interest groups who are seeking some political or social change in some specific political area or areas, but in 2008, the mass public feels a spiritually and emotionally need for political and social change. Whether this great demand for change is a result of the American citizens' distrust, frustration, anger, and lack of confidence in the Bush administration, the prolonged and mishandled Iraq War, record-high gas prices, or and an all-time distrust in our government, one thing is certain: there is a national and international public outcry for the United States of America to change drastically its political direction, political leadership, political philosophies and policies, both domestically and internationally.

There have always been individual citizens, groups of citizens, and organized political and social interest groups that have demanded and argued for change. For example, in the 1960s and early 1970s, there was a public outcry to bring the troops home from Vietnam. During the 1950s and 1960s, blacks demanded change and were granted their civil rights. In the 1980s, the American public demanded change and voted out President Carter and voted in President Reagan because of a great dissatisfaction with Jimmy Carter's handling of the Iranian-hostage crisis and a failing economy that created record-high inflation.

The demand for political and social change is not new and has been in existence since the origin of government, political processes, and political systems. However, 2008 will be the first time in many years that the majority of Americans are seeking one person, the newly elected president of the United States, to lead in creating drastic social and political changes in domestic and foreign policies. American citizens are not just seeking specific changes in certain areas of government, political leadership, education, and the economy; the public seems to be yearning for a change in the political consciousness and political awareness of the nation.

This year, 2008, the American public is seeking more drastic measures of change, not some mediocre changes in policies and laws. American citizens are seeking a level of change that will be great enough to alter the political direction and political thinking of the country. Small change is not sufficient enough for the American public in 2008. Presidential candidates whose arguments do not emphasize change on a great magnitude will fall by the wayside, and those presidential candidates, like Barack Obama, who possesses this special energy of creative and rational political change, will be the public's choice to lead this nation. The year of 2008 will be the beginning of a grand physical, mental, emotional, and spiritual change in our entire political system. Starting with the election of Barack Obama as our new president.

The desire for this higher-level political and social consciousness can be seen in the public's response to Hillary Clinton's candidacy for president in comparison to Barack Obama's candidacy. Both are advocating change; however, Barack has a much greater and higher vision for change than Hillary Clinton. It is not Hillary Clinton's and Barack's policies that are so different, but it is Barack Obama's super political dynamics, high political energy, political consciousness, and political energy awareness that brings about massive and needed changes in a society. Hillary just does not have that high energy, dynamics, and political enthusiasm that Barack naturally and genuinely possesses and expresses. She and her campaign staffers have publicly acknowledged that she is not the dynamic political phenomenon that Barack is.

Even though Hillary Clinton's campaign is attacking Barack on the argument of being too inexperience to be president, the majority of Americans, based on a variety of polls, strongly desire the high-energy level of change that Barack Obama brings to the political arena. This dynamic energy of change that Barack expresses is an intuitive phenomenon that the public senses, likes, and wants to see manifested on a political, social, and governmental level.

I do not doubt that with all of Hillary Clinton's political experience and political talents, she would be a good president. However, I do doubt that she can bring about the kind of drastic and transformational, yet rational and positive change that Barack Obama is articulating and arguing for as he campaigns around the country. Obama has something that Hillary lacks: a natural, an even supernatural, consciousness and a very rare but great political intellect that we Americans have not seen in our leaders in a long time.

Obama has a radiance with his political energy that the other presidential candidates lack. This is a political and personal aura and radiance that will reflect and present an entirely different image of how the world sees the United States. The Obama energy, magnetism, and consciousness can immediately heal the negative reputation and perception that the world has of our great nation.

Politics is more than policy making and passing and signing bills into law. Politics, that is a higher level of politics, is the ability to influence the nation and the world with one's energy, consciousness, and dynamics. Barack Obama possesses these abilities and attributes much more than any presidential candidate.

Hillary Clinton, including her husband, former president Clinton, was nervously sensing that Barack possessed something that they could not reach, verbally attack, or stop. This something is being manifested and grounded in the political world this year and is very spiritual and metaphysical. It is the ability to physically, mentally, emotionally, and spiritually change a social and political energy in a society and to attract masses of people and give them the confidence and hope to envision and create a better nation. Barack Obama's leadership, by itself, will bring about a drastic change in America, because the confidence, hope, inspiration, and motivation that he has given so many Americans are the basis of creating a much greater America.

After all arguments of who will be the best president are fully expressed and argued, the one thing that will separate Barack from Hillary Clinton and all the other Democratic and Republican candidates is that intuitive ability to have the know-how, high political energy and level, and a high intellect to create historic changes in this nation and world. That is the secret weapon that Barack Obama has, and it is this secret gift and ability that has inspired masses of Americans of all races to support and want to elect him as the next president of the United States of America.

However, this book is not an autobiography of Barack Obama's life. Nor is it a book about his specific policies and political plans that he has for the nation when elected president. It is a book about the political energy, consciousness, and awareness that he represents, personifies, and embodies. Barack Obama will be the next president not because of who he physically is but because of the great energy of change and expansive political consciousness and awareness that he has grounded in our nation at this crucial tipping point in our political history.

—Chapter 1—
What He Represents

(What Barack represented was greater than his physical self)

Oprah Winfrey's Endorsement Set the National Tone for Barack Obama

When Oprah Winfrey publicly endorsed Barack Obama's candidacy for president of the United States, she repetitively and decisively said that she endorsed and strongly supported Obama for what he politically and socially represented to this country. Oprah Winfrey's arguments and rhetoric about what Barack Obama represented was very significant, because she understood much more than the on-the-surface politics and typical theatrical presidential campaigning. Oprah immediately recognized that Barack Obama had a new and higher level of leadership that was desperately needed in our nation. Her profound use of the phrase, "What he represents," set the political and social tone of Barack's campaign and his massive political movement of millions of American citizens who have been attracted to his message of hope and creating a better America. "What he represents" became more defined as the presidential campaign intensified and as we approached the presidential election in November 2008.

Oprah's statement that she supported Barack Obama because of what he represented expands the political and social consciousness and energy of Obama. Political consciousness is a political energy that grounds a particular political and social awareness and a higher level of thinking for masses of people. Barack's political consciousness created and grounded a hope, faith, optimism, and confidence across the country like something we had not seen in a many years. He was not just a presidential candidate but a universal representation of a consciousness and political and social movement much greater than his physical self. American citizens were voting for the representation of change, not just for Barack Obama, the man and the Illinois senator. We Americans were not just looking for drastic changes in this nation's leadership and policies but also in the political and social dynamics and energy of this nation's government and politics. By dynamics, I mean the level at which our government inspires and motivates its citizens to participate and create a better political system in our country.

Barack Introduced and Grounded a New Political Consciousness

During the Democratic primary elections, Hillary Clinton confidently and boldly claimed to the American people that she could solve the national and international problems our nation was facing. However, what Hillary and all the other candidates lacked in this campaign was what the majority of Americans were looking for in a candidate. That was a massive political and social energy and enthusiasm to lead this nation and a grounded political consciousness that would emotionally and mentally move the public to envision and create a more advanced America. A more advanced America with a great political system that gives each American the opportunity to achieve that precious national gift: the American dream.

The ability to move American citizens emotionally and politically to take political action to create a much better country and government is the characteristic of great leaders and great leadership. Leadership is more than political problem solving. We, the American citizens, must be motivated and inspired to solve political issues and to push the country's leaders, locally and nationally, to solve political problems and make new, sound-minded, and effective policies and laws.

Increasingly, the public and the political experts are enthusiastically sensing that whatever great political awareness Barack represents, whether it be a conscious or unconscious political and social dynamics or both, will change the political direction of this country. During the 2008 Democratic primaries, the American public chose the great inspiring energy, the political vision, political enthusiasm, and dynamic leadership of Barack rather than the political experience, political skill, and leadership of Hillary Clinton. Later that year, in the presidential election, they chose a high intellectual like Barack Obama over conservative Republican senator John McCain.

The 2008 presidential election was the year that the majority of American voters chose the presidential candidate with the greatest political and social dynamics and high political consciousness, political level, and great vision for the country over the more politically experienced candidate. Even though having extensive political experience in government and politics has its benefits, in 2008, the public was more interested in the ability of a presidential candidate to create a vision for the country and inspire them, the citizens, to help the nation and its leaders fulfill that vision of a better America. The public's frustration with the government, the political system, and the many domestic and international problems reached a boiling and tipping point and made millions of Americans more than willing to take a risk with a more youthful and less-experienced candidate like Barack Obama.

Barack Obama campaigning as a personification of a new political and social consciousness and political energy of change made him a greater candidate than the other candidates, because they did not naturally express that great political aura and political consciousness that Barack and all great leaders have. Barack's political and social consciousness is greater than his physical self. The American public sees Barack's physical self, the man and the presidential candidate. However, they emotionally feel and spiritually see the greater Barack Obama, which is that great energy and political excitement, high level, and amazing dynamics that have made him a national and international political and social phenomenon.

The voters who supported Barack, whether they realized it or not, were voting for the greater side of Barack. This greater side brings a new direction and a higher level of national and international politics, which was Barack's greater side, his great political energy and consciousness that was politically moving and inspiring the country. Oprah Winfrey did not say that she supported Barack Obama because he was black or was a senator from Illinois, nor did she say she supported him because of what he does, has done, or will do. She said that she supported him because he represents and brings an energy of change and hope to this country and personifies a personal, political, and social dynamics and an inspiring political energy. An inspiring political energy that has politically excited the American public more than any political figure in the last fifty years.

Oprah knew that, in our nation's political system, it would take a high consciousness, inspiring and motivating energy, and awareness to make great political and social change. She immediately recognized that Barack Obama, more than any of the other presidential candidates, had all those great qualities that have inspired and motivated millions of American citizens who had never voted in the primary and general elections and became highly interested in participating in their nation's political process.

What Did Barack Represent?

What you represent is the greater you. Representation expands and transcends your physical self, a physical self that is surpassed and transcended by all the things that you represent. What you represent is greater than your lesser humanistical self, a humanistical self that is less than the greater consciousness and awareness that we all have, yet barely use. You are all that you represent, and what you represent defines who you are. You are no greater than what you are representing. Your level of representation defines your greatness, and your greatness is defined by what you represent. The real Barack Obama is what he represents to the country. He represents an expansive and great political energy that has grounded and created a higher political consciousness, political level, and a political vision for the nation. Barack's representation of a new political era is a political phenomenon, a political phenomenon that represents a new kind of political thinking.

Barack had become a candidate of not just government, political issues, and political policies, but a candidate who represented many other great dynamic things. Great leaders reach a leadership level where they symbolize and represent many great things to their nation. Barack

Obama has this level of leadership, a level of leadership that represents a political and social hope, a national pride, and self-confidence for all American citizens.

With representation comes a universal energy, a consciousness, and a motivating and inspiring dynamics. Representation of a political energy or new political consciousness will bring more change than any law or policy, because laws and policies do not motivate and inspire people; what one symbolizes and represents to the nation does motivate and inspire American citizens. For example, Barack represents a new kind of politics for many Americans, and this representation of this new politics in Washington has inspired and motivated people to want to participate enthusiastically in American politics.

What one represents will dictate what kind of political policies one creates. For instance, Barack said that he represented a new political mind-set and a new way of thinking about the war in Iraq. He said a new way of thinking would have prevented the war. This representation of a new way of political and social thinking will influence Barack's Iraq policy, because he promised the American people that, if elected president, he would end as soon and as rationally possible what he called an unjust and unnecessary war.

What one politically and socially represents is also so very influential on the public. For example, Barack represents racial equality, political and social hope for our society, the grounding of the American dream for many Americans, and the transcending of racial, political, and social barriers in our nation. These positive attributes will be felt and seen by the public, and the public will start to receive them as their own. This is the real dynamics of change when a leader's energy emotionally connects with the public and changes the energy and the political and social consciousness and awareness of the public.

Barack's presidency and what he accomplishes as president will reflect what he represents and symbolizes to the country. For example, if Barack represents and symbolizes a national pride, optimism, and a better America, the representation of these positive things will translate into a more politically energized America. Barack Obama's representation of political change and the great energy that accompanies that representation of change will bring more change to this nation than any law or policy, because energy, consciousness, and awareness, unlike laws or policies, inspires, motivates, and moves the public to act and influence the leadership of the country. Barack's great political level and political energy that shines around and from within him is greater than who he is as a senator or politician. His great political and social aura and consciousness that he has politically sown across the country are from his higher political self. That higher self is his high political and social level that has given many American citizens in 2008, one of the worst economic years in recent history, the confidence and hope that they can achieve great things in this great nation.

Barack Obama is a much stronger and more influential and unique presidential candidate as a representative and ambassador of this new political consciousness that created a new political direction for the nation than as a candidate of only policy changes, because the political consciousness is greater than policy making. Policy changes are necessary, but policy changes create a better nation when they are a result of a mass political consciousness and enthusiasm from the American public. Policy changes created by the American public's political inspiration and motivation are politically easier to create and implement and will bring about greater changes than without a massive public movement and national consciousness for change. Policy changes that create more participation of American citizens are much more inspiring and motivating for the country than policy changes that eliminate the participation and decreases the morale of the citizens. Barack Obama knows it is always better for a nation to let the citizens participate, be deeply involved, and have a loud and fair voice in the political system.

The more Barack distanced his argumentation from his physical self as a senator and politician and focused on articulating the political dynamics and political energy that he possessed within, the better chance he had of winning the presidency. American citizens were looking for leaders who had that great and expansive political consciousness and energy. Presenting his expansive political and social consciousness and awareness to the nation was a better and true expression of his greatness and who he was. Barack raised the standard for what it took to be president. Political experience, knowledge, and political skill were no longer enough for the presidency. The American public demanded much more than the boring old politics of the past. American citizens were looking for that great leader, like Barack Obama, who could inspire and bring many more people to participate enthusiastically in the politics and government of our great and constantly aspiring country.

The other presidential candidates, like Hillary Clinton and John McCain, were presenting themselves as mere humanistic presidential candidates, not as a great political consciousness of change like Barack Obama. Presenting oneself only as a candidate and not as a political consciousness or new political awareness limited the greatness of the other candidates. The ability of Barack Obama to express this greater political energy, this greater dynamics and greater consciousness—in essence, this greater part of oneself in the political arena—gives one a higher political level and greater chance of emotionally and politically connecting, motivating, and inspiring American citizens to take action to change, nationally love, take pride in, and improve their government. Hillary Clinton and John McCain were limited in their appeal to the American public, because the nation was looking for that inspirational political energy and political and social dynamics of change Barack naturally expressed. American citizens had enough of the typical, boring, and unenthused politicians who could not inspire or politically excite them about the issues and the political system. The American public was looking for that someone to lead the country, someone with the energy level and the political enthusiasm to solve the many problems facing our nation. Eventually, Barack Obama proved to be this someone.

Barack was a great presidential candidate and potentially will be a great president, because he represents so many great things for our country. His level of representing the many things he symbolizes will determine his greatness. What one represents tells the public what one is all about, what one believes, what one stands for, and what one's commitment and purpose are. The amazing thing about Barack is that he did not necessarily have to tell the American public what he represented to this nation, because they could feel it in his dynamics, aura, confidence, optimism, and political enthusiasm.

Barack Obama represents a political greatness that is much more than himself. For example, Martin Luther King Jr. represented peace, fairness, justice, love for mankind, and racial equality. King's representation of these great universal energies and intangibles of humanity were greater than Martin Luther King Jr. as a physical man. Even Jesus Christ said that he represented and was the embodiment of unconditional love, compassion, and faith, and Christ acknowledged that those intangibles he possessed were greater than his physical self. The great leaders and great people are those who understand that their energy and their level of philosophy and political and social thinking they represent are greater than their name, image, words, or physical selves. Great leaders understand that inspiring and motivating energy and a high energy awareness is the root of the creation of all great historical, political, and social change.

Political dynamics is the creation of the political energy that one represents. Barack Obama, unlike any of the other presidential candidates, had that representation of a new and higher political and social consciousness, representation of the beginning of a new political era and a new kind of political thinking in America. A political thinking that causes people to unite under the common message of making the United States a better country. The common message of hope and a political and social energy that creates great political visions and motivates American citizens to demand and create change.

While Hillary Clinton was saying that she would make changes in the country and world if elected president, Barack Obama was confidently arguing that not only was he going to make changes, he was a personification and embodiment of great political and social changes. That was what Oprah Winfrey was arguing and articulating the weekend that she endorsed and traveled and campaigned across the country with Barack Obama in December of 2007. Barack Obama was finally able to convince the American public that his representation of great and positive change was greater than any political experience that he lacked to be the next president of the United States. He was successful in this argument of change and having a great vision for the country versus his opponents' argument that he lacked political experience in Washington. This was mainly because the American people had reached a political mind-set that having a president like Barack Obama—who focused on changing the political direction, the political and social mentality and thinking of the United States—was more important than having a president who had much political and governmental experience.

A deeper question of the "what he represents" consciousness is what does representing an energy, a dynamics, political level, and philosophy practically mean in the social and political arena? Can the dynamics of what you represent bring about real change where change is needed? Could Barack Obama's representation and personification of change create the kind of change the American public was demanding? Barack Obama's political success was judged and determined by how effectively he argued and emphasized the importance of what he newly represented to our country. The more he distanced himself from being a person and presidential candidate to being a total politically and socially universal consciousness that was fully grounded in our political system, the more mass support he gathered and secured with the voters.

Voters in this presidential election were looking for a change in energy and political dynamics, not only a change in the leaders, policies, and politics. This was best shown in the polls that showed the public was greatly dissatisfied with the political energy and attitude of President Bush, Vice President Dick Cheney, the entire Bush administration, and the Republican Party that have dominated Washington politics the past eight years. Based on a variety of polls, it seemed that American citizens not only wanted the Bush administration to change it policies; it desired a change of energy and a more enthusiastic political attitude as well as policy and leadership changes. That energy change and national political excitement were what Barack Obama personified while campaigning across the country.

A change in the energy and consciousness of politics and government is the key to changing and solving political and social problems quickly and effectively. It is this change in energy and political consciousness and awareness that must occur before the citizens and leaders will see that change is needed. Other presidential candidates had the intellect to argue and articulate change, but they lacked the most important political and social ingredient. That is, the energy, dynamics, and high-level social consciousness that precedes great political changes. The other presidential candidates, such as Senator Hillary Clinton and Senator John McCain, only wanted to change policies and laws, but Barack wanted to first change the total political and social consciousness, awareness, and the way people feel and think about this country. Barack knew that a positive change in the national attitude and mood of the country was the basis of bringing about great changes in this great and powerful nation. After the political consciousness, political awareness, political thinking, political and social attitude of the American citizens and its leaders have changed, great and appropriate policies and laws for our nation will result.

Barack Obama intuitively expresses this inspirational and motivational energy to emotionally move American citizens to demand that the government, both locally and nationally, implement a new and higher level of governing. It is important that the political consciousness, political awareness, and political level of the country be changed first, so that great, sound-minded policies can be created. Creating new and changing old, flawed laws and policies does little good if the consciousness, energy, and political thinking that created those bad policies are not changed first. All policies, whether good or bad, have a political and social energy and dynamics that are responsible for the making of the policy. For example, there was a consciousness and political level behind invading Iraq. To learn the lessons from the Iraq invasion and not make this mistake again, the country, American citizens, and its leaders need to raise drastically their level of political intellect, political awareness, and political consciousness and change the political and social thinking that led us into the war in the first place. Changing the policy of invading Iraq, or invading and going to war with any country without that country being an imminent threat to us, will not be learning the lesson unless the consciousness level of the masses is changed to a higher level. An example of first raising the consciousness level before changing a policy or law will mean that the majority of Americans will have to become passionately aware, motivated, and inspired to pressure their local and national leaders to create our own sources of energy instead of heavily depending on foreign countries, especially the Middle East, to supply us with oil and other energies. Once the majority of Americans reach this high level of political awareness and rational political intellect that will allow us to see that a nation cannot be a total superpower until it is dependent on its own resources and not on foreign oil and foreign energies, the major step of implementing a new policy for this country to create its own energy resources will begin to be realized and achieved. If the dynamics and consciousness for this country to become totally independent of foreign oil is great enough among the public, the biggest oil company, greatest lobbyist, and most stubborn of our political leaders will not be able to stop such a public outcry and political and social movement. The American public was becoming frustrated and puzzling angry about high gas prices. When this massive public anger reached a boiling point, the public became politically and socially aroused, stood up, and spoke out against this issue. This was a political and social boiling point that united the public and grounded a consciousness that started moving the leaders of this nation to create laws and policies that makes this country less dependent on foreign oil and more of a manufacturer of its own energy. Barack Obama intuitively possesses that ability to first raise the consciousness level and then inspire and motivate the public to influence the leaders and politicians to implement these kind of necessary changes in our government.

Another example of political dynamics, political energy, and higher levels of consciousness and awareness preceding the creation of great and historic policy changes was Al Gore's international global warming campaign. Al Gore and many others articulated and created the energy, dynamics, and higher consciousness and awareness about global warming, and that energy and dynamics massively moved the national and international public, leaders, and citizens to take immediate action to prevent the catastrophic results of climate change. As a result of such higher consciousness and awareness of global warming, the fight against global warming has become one of the largest and most influential campaigns in the world, and it has an emotional intensity that is daily attracting and convincing corporations, national and local leaders, and many people worldwide of the imminent and future dangers of global warming and the importance of protecting and saving the planet.

Voters want a president whose energy and aura inspires, motivates, and has a high political enthusiasm, consciousness, and awareness, and a president who creates solutions to problems in the nation and world. A nation and world that is starving for a political optimism and a political and social confidence in its governments and political systems. Barack Obama represents that spiritual and intellectual political dynamics. A spiritual and intellectual dynamics that brings hope for a better future and a better tomorrow, a better tomorrow and a better future that is an inner desire and a national gift to all American citizens who want to create a more enhanced, advanced, and prosperous life for themselves and their children.

—Chapter 2—
The Exception to the Rule

(Experience vs. dynamics)

I learned as a boy how the dynamics of change can be greater than experience when a change of direction is needed. My father was a community league softball coach. At one very important game in the season, his starting pitcher was performing very badly. This pitcher had much experience and had been playing for my dad for many years. However, this day the pitcher's performance was going to cause my dad and his team to lose a major game against a top team in the league. My dad watched on with patience, hoping that maybe this pitcher would emotionally and mentally get it together, throw a few strikes, change the momentum, and eventually win the game. However, that did not happen. The pitcher continued to throw bad pitches until finally, my dad realized that he would have to take this pitcher out of the game if he wanted to have any chance of winning this ball game. My dad replaced this pitcher with a second-string pitcher, who had very little pitching experience in a real game. Not only did this inexperienced pitcher, who was fresh off the bench, perform much better than the first-string pitcher, his presence and energy changed the entire momentum of the game and inspired and motivated the team to come from far behind and win the game.

This example of my dad's team is similar to what is happening in the 2008 campaign and what has happened over the last eight years. The public has been watching this softball game of politics, hoping that the first-string political players will be effective political leaders. The public has been patient for not only the last eight years but the last twenty-five to thirty years, hoping that their political leaders would start pitching good pitches in the political arena.

The American public feels that the softball team of American politics needs a new pitcher who will come into the game, change the momentum of the game, win the game and create a new political and social momentum, change the direction of the political game, and create better policies for the country. The American public is frustrated and has lost confidence in the experienced first-string pitcher, the Bush administration. It is demanding a new pitcher, because American citizens have come to the realization that the starting pitcher, with all of his or her experiences, cannot win this political game. The Bush administration, Senator Hillary Clinton, Senator John McCain, and many of our national leaders and Congress represent the starting pitcher with all the experience, however; Barack Obama is that second-string pitcher who has the energy, dynamics, and inspiration to come into the political game and change the momentum and direction of the political game for our nation.

This comparison of our nation and government to a community softball game may seem a little far-fetched or too simple an example, but it is a perfect parallel to the way the American public views this presidential race, its candidates, and our national leadership. This nation has reached an all-time high of frustration with its leaders and the usual Washington politics. Because of this public's frustration with the national leadership, many Americans have turned to Barack Obama to lead them to a higher level of governing this nation.

Former president Bill Clinton said on *Larry King Live* (CNN) that voting for Barack Obama is like throwing the dice. That is, voting for a presidential candidate who has only been in the U.S. Senate for a year and a half is a big risk for the country. Bill Clinton argues that because this country has never elected a president who has served such a short Senate term and had such little Washington experience, they should not elect Barack Obama. It is arguable whether this is a risk for the American public. One thing is for sure. Because of the many economic and domestic problems facing our nation this year, this is a risk the American people seem willing and free to take. Many American citizens feel it is a bigger risk to continue down the same old road of politics in this country. The same old road of politics that is not solving our nation's problems and is causing the hope of the American people to vanish like vapor in the air.

I do not think it is necessary for me to give arguments why experience is important and advantageous in anything that you do, whether it be in politics, sports, or any aspect of your personal and professional life. However, what experience does not do, as valuable as it is, is create the dynamics that is needed for a change of course and direction in the political arena. The major argument of the 2008 presidential campaign is the experience of Hillary Clinton and the Republican presidential candidates versus the high-level dynamics, consciousness, awareness, energy, and extraordinary intellect and leadership of Barack Obama. The voters will decide what they think is better for the country. Hillary and the other candidates argue that their experience and all of their political and leadership knowledge and political skill will be more efficient than Barack Obama's high-level political energy and an ability to create the dynamics that creates change. Based on many presidential campaign polls and the massive support that Obama has solidified, it appears that the majority of Americas do not agree that Barack Obama's lack of experience will prevent him from being a good and even a great president. What matters is whether Barack can be an efficient president. Does his high political intellect and ability to inspire and motivate the country outweigh his lack of political experience?

Barack Obama has an advantage over his opponents in their argument of his inexperience. First, no one can prove that he will or will not be a good president with or without much experience. For example, none of the other candidates can say that Barack had little experience in some other political job in the past or was the U.S. president in the past, and he did an inefficient job. The public seems to agree with the premise that Barack Obama has shown nothing in his argumentation, rhetoric, or demeanor that indicates that he will not be a very good president. He has actually done the opposite. His opponents futilely tried to trap him when he was hypothetically asked what would he do if he were president and the Pakistani government knew where bin Laden was but refused to turn him over to the United States. Barack said that if all diplomacy failed, the United States would forcefully go into Pakistan and get bin Laden. For a few days, the other presidential candidates tried to argue that Barack's statements were a perfect example of the comments of an inexperienced and immature political leader. However, once it was made clear that Barack was speaking in a hypothetical situation and he would only invade Pakistan after he had exhausted all political and diplomatic means to have bin Laden turned over to the United States, the other candidates had to agree with his rationale. When all the presidential candidates were asked in a televised debate, they said that they would also forcefully go into Pakistan and get bin Laden if the Pakistani government would not turn him over. None of the other candidates could offer any other alternatives to Barack Obama's proposition. This was a very momentous campaign victory for Obama, because at that time, the majority of Americans did not feel that he was ready to lead the country because of lack of experience. However, after that debate, the majority of Americans saw him as efficient, if not more, as the other presidential candidates. The verbal attacks on Barack's inexperience did not stop from the other candidates; however, he eliminated much of the public's doubt that he was more than qualified to be the next president. As far as a president needing much political experience to run this country, Barack proved that he was the exception to the rule.

That leads to the next argument, which is whether an inexperienced person can be as good and effective as a very experienced person. This question can be answered with a yes and no, depending on the circumstances. There are always exceptions to the rule. Everyone probably knows of some instances where the more-experienced person was more efficient than the inexperienced and vice versa. Sometimes one's level of performance, whether it be sports, politics, or any kind of job, may not be based how much experience or inexperience one has, but based on other variables such as one's skill level in that particular field, one's articulation, one's ability to argue, one's diplomatic skills, or one's understanding of how politics works. If one's ability to perform is at a level where performance is more than efficient, then experience is not as important; however, if one's performance is average or below average, then experience becomes more of a necessity.

The old adage says, "experience is the best teacher." This is true; however, it does not take everyone the same amount of experience to achieve results and a certain performance level. Some people need much experience, and others need much less experience. Some of us are slow learners and some are quick learners. It depends on everyone's natural gifts, talents, ambitions, and the speed to absorb information and learnings. Barack Obama is in the category of the quick learner. He has learned an important political lesson that many politicians with many years of experience have not learned. That is, it is the inspiration and motivation of the people that will determine how great a nation will be. It took many NBA players many years of NBA experience before they became good or won championships. However, like Barack Obama, Magic Johnson came into the NBA his first year and helped lead the Lakers to the championship. Politics, like anything else, works the same way. It may take one person twenty years to learn the political lessons that another person, like Barack Obama, could learn in a year and a half. Experience does not necessary breed awareness, intelligence, patience, or great leadership. For example, from the very beginning, Barack Obama courageously opposed the invasion of the Iraq, unlike most of the other presidential candidates, who supported the Iraq war. Barack Obama, the least politically experienced, saw how big of a political, financial, and moral mistake this war was. He showed good judgment from the beginning, while most of the more-experienced Congress members showed bad judgment. Much experience does not necessarily create good and sound judgment, and good judgment does not necessarily need experience. The other candidates said that they voted for the Iraq war because the intelligence said that Saddam was an imminent threat. Even with that kind of intelligence, true or false, floating around Washington, Barack Obama was smart enough to know that this war will go down in history as one of the greatest political mistakes in U.S. history.

The big question is why Hillary Clinton and most of the other presidential candidates did not vote against the Iraq war, because now they all are admitting it was a mistake. Why did all of their political and social experiences and knowledge of the past, which they claim to have more of than Obama, not help them to see the nonsense and foolishness of a war that would be viewed by the world as U.S. imperialism, abuse of power, and an illegal aggression? Why did much experience not tell all these presidential hopefuls that this war would drastically increase our deficit and take us into a recession? Why did much experience not make these presidential candidates, who were so critical of Barack's lack of experience, aware of better alternatives for dealing with Iraq and Saddam

Hussein and becoming independent of Middle Eastern oil? Why did our experienced candidates not realize that those hundreds of billions of dollars spent on the war could have been spent on researching and finding alternative energy so that we would not have to be dependent on the Middle East and need to create a war in order to control energy sources. These questions can be simply answered. A president's judgment is more important and vital than a president's experience. Barack Obama is the answer. That is, much experience does not always solve political problems and create good sound policies and laws. Sometimes a higher intellect, higher political consciousness and awareness, like Obama's, can be the magical solution.

—Chapter 3—
The End and Beginning
of a Political Era

(Change is inevitable)

The year 2008 is one of the beginning and the ending of a political era. It will be the end of the Bush administration and possibly the end of the Republican Party's dominance that has held power since the Reagan years. Dissatisfaction with the Republican Party is the highest it has been in the last fifty years or more, and the public's trust of President Bush and his administration is the lowest of any president since the resignation of President Nixon.

There is a conscious and unconscious desire of the American public for a change of direction for the country. There have always been citizens who have disagreed and wanted change in certain areas of government or in certain policies, but this is first time in recent history that the American public is demanding, hoping, and literally praying for a 360 degree turn in our nation's political direction. Many polls have indicated that most Americans feel that the country is headed in the wrong direction. However, as President Bush and his administration prepares to exit power and government, Barack Obama is arguing to the public that he is the perfect remedy for this political sickness of being off course and that he can politically steer the nation in a direction that will make our nation a greater nation and greater superpower in the world.

While President Bush, Vice President Dick Cheney and the Bush administration have angered, disengaged, and showed poor diplomatic skill with other world leaders, Barack Obama is confidently articulating that he is the best presidential candidate to heal our diplomatic relations around the world. The Bush administration's policies have created very negative dynamics nationally and internationally and have pushed the public to the opposite side of the Bush administration. The public rejected the conservative ideology of the Bush administration and decided to go with high rationalism, very sound policy making, high-level problem-solving skills, a very high political intellect, and the willingness and energy to make changes. Barack Obama personifies this side of politics, a side of politics that American citizens will welcome with open arms.

As this 2008 presidential campaign starts to unfold, it will be obvious that Barack Obama has one big advantage over all the other candidates. While all the other candidates represent the old era of politics and the end of it, Barack Obama represents the new era, and the American public senses that Barack will be the better candidate to carry the new torch of leadership. The main argument that will determine the next president will be that the old era of politics has become inefficient and who is the best candidate to lead this new era of politics. If the American public believes that this is a transition year of the old to the new and embrace the new, Barack Obama will be the next president of the United States.

More than any of the other presidential candidates, Barack Obama has benefited from the American public's political and social distancing from and distrust of the Republican Party. The unpopularity of the Republican Party has caused many voters, even Republican voters, to open their ears to Barack Obama's message of high political change. The negative stigma and negative image that the Bush adminstration has passed on to the Republican Party is igniting a movement for change not only of ideas and policies but also a change of Republican Party control and power. Even many Republicans are dissatisfied with the present Republican Party policies and philosophies. The majority of Americans blame the Republican Party for the Iraq war, extremely high gas prices, and a failing economy. The Bush administration and the Republican Party may not even realize the extent of the political damage that has been done to the Republican Party, and it may take twelve to sixteen years to heal and reverse the bad image that is now attach to the party and to anyone who is a Republican.

The great consciousness of change that Barack Obama articulates is going to force the Republican Party to make drastic changes in its platform now and in the next few years. If the Republican Party does not make these drastic changes in its conservative platform, it will lose many of it voters to the Democratic Party, or they could become independent voters. The year 2008 and the years to follow are going to change the political climate so much that if the Republican Party refuses to change its outdated platform, it may become a small minority party or even become extinct. In the next few years, the key to survival of any political party in our country will be to change to a high political level or politically die in its old ways. The public is going to demand this change. Why is this? Because there is a new consciousness and new political awareness of no political nonsense and a high rationalism that will ground our nation. Barack Obama is the leader and messenger of this new level of rationalism.

The American public is demanding an end to the old and a start to the new. There is a very rational thinking being voiced from the public about the necessity of change that Barack Obama articulates. American citizens feel that they have been patient with its government and leaders for many decades, and the public has come to a point where it feels it knows what works and what does not work. In all fairness to the government and its leaders, the public has given the leaders and the system time to work things out; however, the public has reached a point of not just frustration with but also lack of confidence in the political system.

The year 2008 will be the beginning of the American public's demand that its political leaders change the old domestic and foreign policies that have not worked and replace them with new policies. American citizens have reached a point of being willing to try new policies rather than continue down the road of prehistoric policies that have not been good for our nation or political system. A perfect example of this will be the implementation of an affordable health-care system. Most polls show that the majority of Americans to want affordable health care. American citizens have reached a point where they feel that if the U.S. government can spend billions upon billions of dollars on the war in Iraq, the country might as well spend billions on an affordable health-care system that will benefit all American citizens. The public demand that the government create an affordable health-care system is an example of how a different level of political and social consciousness can change American citizens' perspective on a political or social issue. The creation of an affordable or universal health-care system will be the beginning of a new system and the ending of an old one. The American public is ready to experiment with some form of affordable or universal health care. The Republican Party has finally lost this argument on affordable and universal health care. They did not lose the argument just to Barack Obama, but they lost to the consciousness of change and the energy of political intelligence. The American public had patiently given the Republican Party a chance to create an efficient health-care system and they failed. American citizens are now willing to give the Democratic Party the chance to implement a new, more affordable, universal health-care system. The consciousness of the public is that this nation needs to try something before we write it off as bad and ineffective, and that definitely applies to the universal health-care issue. The leader of our nation using their political intellect to implement a universal health-care system is the beginning of a new political grounding in this country, and not allowing the big pharmaceutical companies to prevent universal health care will be the end of an old system controlled by big-time lobbyists. This advance political grounding in our nation is a consciousness of good, sound thinking and very high-level problem solving. Barack Obama, more than any other presidential candidate, has this political problem-solving ability and political skill, and it is this political talent and energy that will direct this country not only back on course but to a higher and better political level.

Barack is the ending and the beginning. The ending of the silly waste-of-time bickering politics in Washington and the beginning of smart, strategic, wise politics and decision making that will increase our diplomatic, political, and economic strength around the world and make the lives of all American citizens socially and economically better. The theme of the 2008 election is the ending and the beginning. The ending of doing what is politically irrational and detrimental for our country and the beginning of making highly intelligent, wise, and sound decisions that will greatly enhance our nation. The ending of always being a superpower that always has a national economic deficit and the beginning of being a country that has no national deficit or national debt. The ending of a nation that is dependent on foreign oil and energy and the beginning of being a real superpower, one that creates its own energy and is constantly researching and creating new alternative energy sources. Anything is politically possible when the entire nation changes its political philosophy and political mind-set. Barack Obama has that mind-set for this new political frontier, and he possesses the ambition to make this country a greater and much more all-around superpower. That is, a superpower whose power is not only judged by the size of its military and economy but also on the level of high political intellect and leadership that will help this nation to use its mighty power in the best and highest level possible.

The era of the ending and the beginning is a high consciousness and high awareness for the need for political and social change. American citizens' frustration with our political and social system has created this consciousness of change. Change is the ending followed by a new beginning. An ending not followed by a beginning cannot produce change. A beginning of something without the ending of something else cannot produce change. Barack Obama, more that any other presidential candidate, is the best personification, representation, and manifestation of the ending, beginning, and the great miracle of the energy of change. This new era is crucial, because it will set the tone for our nation's politics and government for many years to come.

—Chapter 4—
Timing Is Everything

(It is Barack Obama's time)

There is nothing like being in the right place at the right time and being that special person for that special occasion or special purpose. When the time and the person come together, this a perfect harmony for change and the creation of a political and social newness. When the person and the purpose become one, this produces changes of a great magnitude that create a totally new direction of government and politics in a nation, a government and politics that will create a great respect between American citizens and their government. A mutual respect that will cause the government to make policies that will help American citizens in every aspect of their lives.

Barack Obama is coming into the political arena at the right time. The right time is this year of 2008. It is the year that Barack Obama's energy of newness and change is the same as the American public's desire for change. The public's desire for change is what Barack embodies, and what Barack embodies is the hope, new, and fresh leadership that bring our nation's politics to a higher level. Once our national political thinking reaches this high level, all citizens can reap the benefits of a politically and socially prosperous country.

This is the time for change. Not tomorrow, but today. For today is the oneness of the Barack Obama phenomenon and the American public's enthusiasm to move the nation forward. This oneness with the

American public will create a new enthusiasm and public inspiration, which will result in a new direction for the nation. This new direction will eliminate the out-of-control gas prices, restore the housing market, finally stabilize Iraq, bring stability back to our economy, and eliminate poverty and ghettos in America. Among all the presidential candidates, Barack Obama is the only one who has become one with the thinking of the majority of the American people. Becoming one with the thinking of American citizens allows Barack to empathize with each citizen and present a pathway to change that will allow each citizen to benefit from the political and social changes that he will bring to the table of politics. This table of politics will allow each citizen to have an opportunity to share in the riches, freedom, and prosperity of this country. This prosperity is what change is supposed to bring. A change that we Americans expect as citizens.

Why is 2008 the year for change? Why are other presidential candidates, in addition to Obama, advocating change in some form? Is change just a reflection of the time we are living in? Does the American public have a need and desire for change because of the many problems our nation is facing? Is change that inevitable consciousness and dynamics that naturally occurs, or do we, the American citizens, take the iniative to create the change? There are many questions and answers that can be given about change and what causes people to embrace the energy of change. However, the energy that Barack Obama has demonstrated shows that he is in alignment with the time, the purpose at hand, and the political and social energy to bring about those necessary changes in our political system.

Throughout history when change was needed, there was always that right soul that the universe chose to fulfill that purpose. That purpose could be spiritual, religious, political, or social. These special souls have been called everything from messengers, saviors, prophets, chosen ones, special people, and even divine ones. No matter what one would call these purposeful individuals, they always fulfilled their mission and were the perfect match and calling for the mission at hand. Even if they become martyrs, they are highly efficient and committed to their purpose, and it becomes obvious that he or she was sent to the earth for that purpose. Jesus Christ, Martin Luther King Jr., and Gandhi are good examples of how the person, the purpose, and the time all come together to create a massive change in politics, religion, or any aspect of society. Barack Obama, the youngest of all the candidates, is running for president of the United States at the right time with the right message and the right purpose. The time is change. The message is change. The purpose is change.

Time is more than the element of the movement of energy that lets us know where we are in the minute, the hour, the day, the week, the month, the year, the decade, the century, the millennium, and the era. Time dictates our beliefs, whether they be political, moral, or social. For example, what one believed was morally right one thousand years ago one may not believe is morally right today. The advancement of human rights and animal rights are good examples of how time can change the awareness and consciousness of people. Black slavery is another example. In the past, there were many people who did not feel that slavery was wrong. It was the norm, and many thought it was a legitimate necessity. Time is going to play a big part in this 2008 election, because what people were seeking from candidates at other times is going be very different from what the American public is seeking today. Barack Obama and time have become one. American government and American politics have become one with time. Politics and government change with time. Barack Obama's presidential candidacy is perfect timing, and all his political and social philosophies and dynamics of change are the product of time.

Time creates change. Time creates the awareness and the consciousness that are needed to make change on a political and social level. Time creates the opportunity for change. This opportunity for change is a combination of the desire for change from the public and its leaders. The opportunity for change is now, and Barack Obama has synchronized with the American public's desire for change. This synchronization with the public's desire for change will make change happen quicker and harmoniously. When there is no agreement for change from the leaders and their citizens, then things such as protest and other forceful means are necessary to bring about change. Election 2008 will not require any forceful means from leaders or protests from the public to bring about change, because this is a year of the oneness of change and time. Time creates change, and change creates a new time, a new time of new political and social perspectives and new levels of governing this great nation. Every American citizen will feel in the air that it is time to change many things in our great political system.

Barack Obama is a product of time, not of Washington politics. Obama knows that 2008 is his year to become president of the United States. Not four or eight years from now. Now is the time, because Barack, more than any other presidential candidate, has time on his side. In this presidential election, time is greater than any experience, any campaign ad, any political argument, rhetoric, well-written speech, or any public or private endorsement.

The timing of Barack Obama is no coincidence. In timing, there is no coincidence or luck. Timing eliminates luck and coincidence, for timing is everything. It is the person, the message, the purpose, the change, the dynamics, the level, the awareness, and the end result; all are within the realm of perfect timing. Perfect timing in politics is what American citizens desperately want. Perfect timing in politics is when the leaders and the citizens are on the same political page and come together to create and build a greater nation. We, the Americans citizens, know that it is time to change our leadership and the way we have been doing politics in this country. American citizens desire a change of leaders, a change of the leader's thinking, a change of the failing policies and ineffective laws of our country. Barack Obama's appearance on the political scene is perfect timing. A perfect timing that brings hope. This hope is also a product of this perfect realm of timing that has positively infiltrated America and demands immediate and drastic changes in our political system.

Time brings new changes, but it ends an old system, old habits, old thinking, old philosophies, and old policies. Time lets go of the past as well as holds onto the future. The American public has reached a point in this energy of time when they are convinced that it is better to let go of the past and go in a different direction than continue down the same path of political, economic, and social deterioration and destruction. Time has convinced American citizens that a future with new ideas is a much better America than to continue in the old direction of ineffective and stagnated ideas that decrease the inspiration and motivation of our nation.

Time awakens individuals. Time awakens people. Time awakens nations. Time brings new ideas, new learnings, new teachings, creativity, and new levels. Time creates a new hope for yesterday, today, and tomorrow. Time changes the minds of leaders and citizens and inspires them to participate equally in the political system. Time changes the minds of stubborn leaders and makes them search their intellect for a higher level of political and social thinking that will enhance our political system. Time creates democracies and makes present democracies better democracies. Time gives people hope and confidence that they can have and live a richer life, a more prosperous and fulfilling life as citizens of this great country. Time moves people to act and to act with patience and sound-mindedness. The year 2008 is not just the year of the presidential election and change. It is the year of the grounding of the energy of time in our political and social system.

Barack Obama represents time. The time to win a presidential election and to be the leader of a nation that needs changes in how it solves its problems. Barack Obama symbolizes and he is a personification of time. Time to change the tarnished reputation of America around the world. Barack Obama is a creation of time. Time to create a political system that is fair to the rich, middle class, poor, business, and corporations. Barack Obama is a messenger of time. Time to articulate a message of economic, social, and political hope and a grounded vision of the American dream for every citizen.

Time is reality, not just rhetoric and well-spoken words. Time creates action and that action creates the needed changes that we Americans are longing to have in our political system. Time is constantly moving and is not stagnated and stuck in ignorance, closemindedness, and arrogance. Time is constantly thinking of how to make things better. Time is willing to change and is not afraid of drastic changes. Time is opportune with the message, the messenger, and the purpose. Time is ready to embrace our political system and to enlighten our political leaders and give American citizens a vision of how the nation can be a much safer and greater nation in all political, economic, social, and every other area that is of utmost importance to the American citizen. Time can never be wrong, because when decisions are made within the realm of perfect timing, it will create a harmonious result that is beneficial to our nation, our citizens, and the world. Barack Obama came with time, and time came with Barack. Now we, the American citizens, must accept this great phenomenon, the Barack Obama level and energy. Barack Obama, whom time has brought to the table of higher political learning, will be able to feast and dine with

American citizens and celebrate a new political era and a more highly advanced America.

—Chapter 5—
Transcending Race

(Barack, as U.S. president, is the perfect healer of racism)

This chapter is one of, if not the most important and significant chapters in this book. Transcending race is such a high-level learning, dynamics, and such a social and political necessity needed in our nation, that I could write an entire book on this chapter. The ability to transcend your race and all races, and what that creates in a multiracial society, is very important in the political and social arenas. This chapter will not only explain how Barack Obama's political achievements to run for president and eventually become president enhanced the American public's ability to transcend race, racial differences, and barriers. This chapter also analyzes how his personal dynamics caused him to attract people of different races and allow them to not only fully accept him as a black man but to accept him as a leader and a political phenomenon much greater than race and skin color. This something is the power of racial unity and the message of making racial America a nonracial America. It will be this power of racial unity that will raise this entire nation to a level where racism and ignorance cannot exist.

On March 18, 2008, Barack was fully challenged on his ability to recognize, address, and unify the races in the country. After a politically grueling week of being questioned and attacked by the media and the conservatives in the country for his twenty-year close friendship with his pastor, Reverend Jeremiah Wright, who had been know to express publicly many racist and anti-American remarks. In an unprecedented televised speech, Barack Obama did what no other leader or politician had done in the country. He fully and directly addressed the race issue in this country by speaking to all races. Barack's speech not only showed that he had the ability to correctly assess the race relations of the country but that he had the leadership and the needed rhetoric to unify all races and help them transcend all racial barriers. Racial barriers that kept this country caught in a prehistoric world of great racial ignorance.

It is important that I clarify the definition of transcending race. The word transcending means to rise above and to go up and beyond. Transcending one's race does not mean hating one's race or being ashamed of one's race or other races. Everyone should be proud of and love his or her ethnicity, skin color, and specific physical characteristics. One must first love one's race and other races before one can rise above the whole race factor. Transcending race is becoming aware, like Martin Luther King Jr., that even if races look different, everyone is a human being who shares the same needs. Transcending race is reaching a level where you know it is nonsense to judge someone by skin color or ethnicity instead of by character, morals, and personal values and behavior. Transcending race can be simply defined: it is rising above the racial hatred, biases, prejudices in which we human beings can become susceptible. Barack Obama has risen and reached that level of total racial consciousness and awareness.

The ability to transcend race genuinely is not an easy thing for most people, especially presidential candidates and politicians. Many people think transcending race is avoiding talking about race or racial problems. That is fear of race, not transcending race. Transcending race is the freedom to communicate fully and honestly with all races with no negative judgments based on skin color or ethnicity. When one transcends race, one sees other races as one sees one's own race: as fellow human beings who should be treated and loved as you want to be treated and loved. Barack Obama has that ability to communicate and bring all races together under the common message of let's transcend to a higher racial level, higher racial consciousness, and higher racial awareness of racial unity that will make this nation a greater nation for the citizens of every race.

Transcending race requires that one be at a high level of awareness of one's own race and that one's dynamics and energy are greater and above all racial differences. Transcending race is recognizing that everyone has something in common that is greater than any racial differences. For example, a message about the energy of hope transcends race and racial differences, because who, at some time or other, has needed and desired hope, no matter what your race or skin color is. White individuals, as well as black people and other races, need hope. All people, of all ethnicities and nationalities, need and desire the energies of love and hope. People of all walks of life want prosperity, and Barack Obama, with his message of hope, represents that change to a more prosperous life for all races in the United States of America.

Barack Obama's message of change definitely transcends race, because change is a universal energy that everyone yearns to have. Barack's high-level message of change causes people to forget what color his or her skin or ethnicity is. The American public's desire for change is much greater than how it sees Obama's race or skin color. The majority of Americans see Barack Obama as a leader of change, not a black man running for president. What Barack was and is able to do is something that Al Sharpton and the Reverend Jesse Jackson were not able to do. That is, make the majority of Americans do what Martin Luther King Jr. said in his "I have a dream" speech: judge Barack Obama not by the color of his skin but by the content of his character and his ability to lead this great nation.

Barack Obama's high-level arguments, rhetoric, and philosophy have caused the public to respond by raising their level of racial awareness and racial consciousness. Barack's transcending of race caused the majority of Americans to transcend race in this presidential election year of 2008 and elect him president. This transcending of race by the public caused them to hear the higher political level and consciousness that Barack articulated. Racism cannot exist in this higher political and social consciousness and awareness. Barack's message of change is raising the level of the American public's social and political intellect. A political and social intellect that understands that racism is the worst political and social disease for this great nation.

As time goes on, more people in our country will embrace this high racial awareness that Barack Obama has helped to ground in our nation. All will not embrace it at once; however, 2008 will be the beginning of a new racial level and racial philosophy in our country. A new racial level and racial philosophy that will politically and socially advance our country to a genuine and sincere level of racial peace. A level of racial peace and harmony where all races will learn to respect, communicate, and work together without silly and ignorant racial mistrust and suspicion. This is the transcending that Martin Luther King Jr. dreamed would happen. Barack Obama is a manifestation and grounding of this dream and this new level of racial transcending.

Obama's transcending rhetoric and message of change will still greatly influence those hateful and subtly racist people, because racial ignorance and low racial awareness cannot coincide with a higher racial awareness and a higher racial consciousness. Barack is not just preaching change. His dynamics and aura is bringing change to this nation. The transcending image of this highly intellectual, dynamic, young presidential candidate, who articulates a message that hits the gut of the most racist of people, will in the long term win those lost souls. The energy of transcending race, the energy of higher racial awareness, and the energy of higher racial consciousness will eventually embrace those racist souls and raise their minds to a level of racial tolerance and love for their fellow American citizens. Barack makes all people, racist and nonracist, feel that they are worthy American citizens with dreams that can be fulfilled in this great country. History has proven that racism can be healed, and Barack is living proof of this healing.

An Obama presidency will do something that was very difficult for Martin Luther King Jr. to do. Martin Luther King Jr. transcended race with his high love for mankind, his great intellect, and the "I have a dream" speech, but it was very difficult, because of that time, to get the majority of Americans, even blacks, to transcend race and racial barriers. There was too much hatred in the country, from both blacks and whites, for Martin Luther King Jr. to convince and mentally take the American public to this higher racial consciousness. With all of Martin Luther King Jr.'s great and historic civil rights achievements, the transcending of race and racial barriers in America was something he could only hope, dream, and pray would happen someday.

That someday is now, and Barack Obama is the total fulfillment of King's dream of seeing all people, especially an Afro-American, judged and accepted based on who he or she is as a person and not skin color. Martin Luther King Jr. would have been so happy to see all the multiracial crowds of people excitingly supporting Barack Obama, listening and accepting his message of a new and better tomorrow and an end to an unhopeful yesterday. Barack transcends race, because his message and energy takes people to such a high level of intellect and great political and social thinking. Great political and social thinking where racial differences do not matter, and racial hate and prejudice cannot exist.

Barack Obama's natural gift to unify a racially diverse nation under one message of change is a phenomenon in itself. His message, his dynamics, his energy of change is transcending political party barriers as well as racial barriers. Even many Republican voters are supporting Obama in this presidential election. The political level, high intellect, and political reasoning of Barack Obama have helped people to see that the problems of our nation and world help people to see that one's race and skin color are not what solves political problems. It is the person's leadership and his or her political skill and innovative ideas that will solve our nation's and world's problems. It is one's ability to bring about change that is going to create a better government and better nation for all American citizens, not one's race. One's race is not going solve the national debt, the war in Iraq, our national economic problems, terrorism, and the many problems facing our world, but the high rational and sound political thinking that Barack Obama possesses is what will solve political problems and transcend the entire nation above all racial differences.

This level and dynamic ability of Barack Obama to transcend race is more than a benefit to race relations in this country. This racial transcending has a more universal meaning. His ability to rise above all racial barriers and to convince voters on a conscious and unconscious level to transcend racial differences and racial barriers is representative of an higher level of transcending. That is transcending old political and social ways of thinking, transcending ineffective ways of doing politics and governing this country, transcending a resistance and fear of change for what is best for our nation, and finally, transcending an unhopeful life as an American citizen to a prosperous, optimistic life that is fulfilling in every aspect for the American dream.

—Chapter 6—
Prophecy, History, and Destiny Cannot Be Stopped

(The Obama phenomena is a creation of the political universe)

The year 2008, the year of conscious and unconscious changes in our political and social thinking, is also the grounding and the manifestation of political and social prophecy, destiny, and history. The Obama phenomenon is the prophecy. The Obama phenomenon is the destiny. The Obama phenomenon is the history. It is the year of black history and American history. The prophecy is the Barack presidential candidacy, his message for change and the greatness of our nation that follows this political and social change. The prophecy is also the fulfillment of the dreams, tiring prayers, and endless hope of Martin Luther King Jr., many other black leaders and blacks who sacrificed their lives for an Afro-American like Barack Obama with the hope that someday, an Afro-American would become president of the United States. The destiny is what will be will be and what is going to be. That is, Barack Obama is going to be the next president of the United States of America. The history is that Barack Obama will not only be first Afro-American to become president, but he will lead one of the most historical movements of rational and sounded-minded change in recent history of this country.

Throughout history, there have been leaders who came, led a political or social movement, helped create positive changes, and left a lasting impact on a nation and the world. Barack Obama is such a leader. He leads the political movement of change and is sure to leave a lasting impact on our nation. Barack is one of the most unique presidential candidates in our nation's history, because if elected president, he will bring the support of an entire political movement of change that he built while campaigning across the country. Even the voters who were supporting other presidential candidates were attracted to this dynamic energy of change that Barack Obama expressed around the country. This was evident in that many of the presidential candidates were also preaching a message of change, because they saw how many millions of people were drawn to Barack's message of hope and change.

Obama is history in the making. He is past history, present history, and future history. He is past history, because he represents the great changes that have been made in the past to help make this a great nation. He is present history, because presently he is moving masses of people to want to make great political and social changes in the country. Barack is future history, because he will be remembered as the presidential candidate and president who led a nationwide movement of change that consisted of enthusiastic American citizens who were inspired and wanted to see the country dream bigger and do better things.

Was Barack destined to be the president of the United States? As the campaign continued, many of the other presidential candidates were fearfully starting to sense that Obama was destined to win. The American public was starting to sense that it was inevitable that Barack would win the presidency. Was he put on this earth to be president? Is that his main purpose on planet earth? Was Barack born to lead our country like Michael Jordan and Magic Johnson were born to play basketball? Was Barack destined the be the only Afro-American in U.S. history to become president of this great nation, like Muhammed Ali was born to be a great boxing champion. The wind was blowing, and it blew Barack and his energy of change into the White House.

Barack has found history, and history has found Barack. Barack has found destiny, and destiny has found Barack. Barack has found prophecy, and prophecy has found Barack. These three energies of history, prophecy, and destiny were more than just about Barack as a presidential candidate. The history, destiny, and prophecy, which were long overdue, were the grounding of a political and social consciousness that turned our nation in the right political direction. This political and social consciousness is what every American citizen so deeply desires. That is, the grounding of the history, destiny, and prophecy of the American dream. The American dream is the full manifestation of total happiness in every walk of life of each American citizen. With the American dream is the freedom to advance your total self, freely take risks, and take advantage of opportunities to better your life and the life of your family.

The reality that Barack could become president was when he won the Iowa caucus. That killed Hillary Clinton's perception of being invincible, and it gave Barack and his campaign the confidence and faith to believe that a Barack Democratic domination and presidency could really happen. This win in Iowa encouraged the Barack supporters that they were not futilely believing in a fake consciousness but in a real level of high political energy and dynamics. This first win for Barack also awakened the nation to the fact that there was a new phenomenon in the political arena, a political and social phenomenon that was destined to get bigger.

The other presidential candidates, with all of their campaign strategies, campaigning experience, and talents, were up against a political force that they were not able to compete against. This political force was the Obama prophecy, destiny, and history, which were the winning factors that campaign strategists and political experts probably did not factor into their campaign strategy. This powerful spiritual and political aura that surrounds Barack Obama, even though unseen, could be strongly felt and heard across the country. The American public sensed that this Barack Obama phenomenon might be something much greater than a presidential candidate trying to win votes to get into the White House. American citizens started to feel a new consciousness and energy that had not politically and socially swept the nation off its feet in many years. The other candidates had been feeling that Barack was driven by this spiritual and political energy that they did not have. The other candidates were surprisingly overwhelmed by the massive and universal dynamics that Barack was pouring out to millions of American citizens throughout the country. The other presidential candidates wanted to lead this great social and political consciousness that grounded in the nation in 2008. They could not, however, because they lacked that high political level, political energy, and extraordinary political dynamics that Barack Obama had.

Destiny cannot be stopped. What is behind this political force that has pushed Barack Obama into the political spotlight? Why could this energy not be stopped by other candidates' strategies, rhetoric, arguments, and verbal attacks? Why did the American public support Barack Obama all the way to the national election polls? Why did this message of change not die like a withering flower but bloomed into a fulfilled prophecy? If it was not for Barack to be president, he would not have become president. However, in destiny there is no if. There is only the fulfillment of destiny, and that is what the 2008 election manifested and fulfilled. Only time can control destiny, and the time is now.

Destiny is a production and creation of time. Barack has been patiently waiting for this moment. The American public has been waiting for this historical moment, which is the grounding of a national change in political philosophy. This moment is part of the political destiny of not only Barack Obama but of the United States of America. The political destiny of this country is to be a nation that will continue to strive to the highest levels in every aspect of government, politics and education. This striving to the highest levels as a nation is also to see that all American citizens are given the fair opportunity to get to that higher level of total living as an American. That higher level of total living is not just monetary and educational; it is a mental, emotional, and spiritual level that gives one a total prosperity. This total prosperity is the true destiny of our great nation and the true fulfillment, manifestation, and creation of the American dream.

History will always continue to bring new, great, and innovative leaders into this country and world. History working in harmony with time always delivers these great leaders at the right time and right place. Barack Obama is a production of the great history. He is the past history, present history and future history, all created inside one man.

Past history is the history of how we as a nation have progressed to this present level of political awareness. This country has come a long way, and Barack Obama's great success as a presidential candidate and his leadership of this great movement of change was a great and perfect manifestation of the progress of past history. A past history that was stagnated in political racism and discrimination. The progress of past history was shown in the many white voters and supporters who were willing to transcend race and accept Barack Obama as the first black American president. Past history has evolved and created this great movement of change, because it is this past energy of change that has continued to allow our nation to advance and flourish as a nation.

Present history, which is a new advanced creation of past history, is the action that our nation and leaders are taking to improve the country, both politically and socially. This year of 2008, one of the most exciting presidential elections ever, is an example of present history. Present history learns from and improves past history. Barack Obama is bringing a present history to this country that will change policies, change political minds, and change how we as American leaders and citizens think about our government and politics. It is in this present history that this nation will act to change, energize, move, and advance this country to the next levels of higher government. It is this next level of higher government that will prepare this country for the future. It is this brighter future that is a creation of the present history. A present history, which will one day be past history, is preparing the nation for the future history. A future history for our children and grandchildren that will help them reach the highest levels of living as an American citizen.

The future history of our country is the future that is created by our past and present actions. Barack Obama represents and leads this future history, because his great message of change and moving to a higher level of consciousness and awareness is setting the tone for the future and is the beginning of creating a better government for the future. The future history can only be created when we, as nation, have learned the political lessons of the past and present. Once we have learned the political lessons of the past and present, we can create a better way of politics in our country. A better way of politics that will inspire and motivate all Americans, young and old, to participate in this new, advanced political system and happily and joyfully be part of the new age of political advancement and political enlightenment.

—Chapter 7—
The Greatest Argument

(Barack's arguments for change are the most valid in recent history)

Barack Obama's main argument during his presidential campaign was the argument for drastic and effective change in American politics and government. This argument was a reflection of American citizens' demand and desire for changes in their government and political system because of the public's perception combined with the stark reality of the financial problems that were economically paralyzing the country. This combination of real problems and the American public's perception of these problems and issues created a national anger and frustration with the government and its leaders. The reality and the public's negative perception of the crumbling stock market, massive loss of many ordinary American citizens' retirements and investments, and a deepening economic recession created a momentous opportunity for Barack Obama to argue nationally that he was the better leader to bring about the change that we Americans wanted.

The argument for change helped Obama attract millions of supporters, and most Americans—Democrats, Republicans, and Independents—felt that the government and its leaders needed to make policy changes and govern differently. Throughout the country, people have expressed much dissatisfaction with the extremely fragile economy, its deficit and national debt, the Iraq and Afghanistan wars, the collapsing housing market, record-high gas and energy prices, extremely high unemployment, and a very negative perception of how the world viewed the United States. These were, and are, real problems, and the American public sees them as real problems that need to be solved. American citizens intellectually and emotionally believed in the urgent need for change that Barack Obama had nationally argued during his campaign. Daily, he articulated that he was the leader who had the level of political energy and political intellect to bring about these short- and long-term changes that would improve our nation and direct us back on course to national prosperity.

The public's negative perception of the government and political parties should not be underestimated. During the 2008 presidential election, the Republican Party suffered a devastating political defeat. A politically crippling defeat that was created not just by the American public's negative perception of the Republican Party but by the real problems that our nation was facing. This negative national public perception of the Republican Party resulted in the election of President Barack Obama and a Democratic majority in the Congress and was created by real problems that had occurred during a Republican administration led by President Bush. The public's negative perception resulted from the negative reality of the worst financial crisis since the Great Depression and the collapsing financial system. The American public's negative perception was created by the reality of massive economic problems and political issues. What the public perceives is the perceptive reality. Perceptive reality is the reality created by the public's perception, which is the reality as American citizens see it.

Perception and reality are different; however, they can become one when the public's perception accurately reflects the reality that the public sees, and the reality, positive or negative, accurately reflects the public's perception. For example, there was a negative perception in this country that President George W. Bush led this country in the wrong political direction, both domestically and internationally. This was a reality and a perception, because the reality is that this country is experiencing some of the worst problems that it has experienced in many decades, and even if President Bush and his administration were not the blame for all these problems, most happened during his two terms, and some were, especially his foreign policies, detrimental to the image of the United States and our diplomatic relations with other countries. This negative reality created a negative public perception, which was that President Bush was leading the nation in the wrong direction. That perception, right or wrong, biased or unbiased, was what the American public believed, felt, and saw as real.

These concepts of perception and reality were relevant to Barack Obama's rise to political power in America, because whether it was the failing economy or a prolonged Iraq war, these big national and international problems created a political perception of failed policies. The public's negative political perception became one with the negative reality. That negative reality was the failed policies by the Bush administration and a Congress, both Democrats and Republicans, that seemed incompetent to deal with the national and international financial crisis. For example, the public perceived that the government had failed them, and this perception was substantiated by the reality of a government that appeared unable to return the financial system to normality and unable to solve many other problems with the interest of the people at heart. Both the public's perception and reality became much worse as a result of each other. Because of the negative public perception, American citizens lost confidence in the government's ability to solve national and international problems in a highly sound-minded and practical way. The reality became worse as a result of a worsened perception, because the people's lack of confidence in the financial and political system caused them to reject and not participate in the system, and this worsened the problem. For instance, if a small-business owner perceives that the economy is bad and wholesale inflation is rising, he or she may decide not to hire new employees and even worse, lay off present employees. Laying off and not hiring employees drastically slows the economy, which adds to the reality of a economic recession. This worsened reality then adds to the negative perception of the small-business owner, who reacts to the reality with a higher negative perception. Another example is that if the reality is that the banking system is in trouble and the public perceives that the banking system is in trouble, the public may do things like withdraw their money from the bank, not invest in banking markets, or not take out a loan from a particular bank. Another example of how perception and reality can affect each other is with consumer spending.

If the consumers perceive that the economy is not good and the reality is that the economy is not doing well, the consumers may drastically reduce how much money they spend. When the consumers stop spending, it is very detrimental to a healthy economy. A negative consumers' perception of the economy created by the negative reality of an unstable economy creates even a more unhealthy economy, and this creates a more negative public perception of the economy. This cycle of perception influencing what is real and what is real influencing perception can be an endless cycle, and it created the massive public demand for change that this nation and the world saw in our 2008 presidential election. The American public's need for change is rooted in a political perception, a political reality, or both, and these political and social perceptions and realities caused this nation, American citizens, to rise politically and socially and demand that its leaders make drastic changes in the way that they govern the country and to change to a higher philosophy of politics, policy making, and governing. Understanding the public's perception and the reality that the public sees is very important in understanding how Barack Obama's argument for change was not only based on the negative national and international realities but also on the negative public perception that was created by the real problems and issues of our nation.

A negative political reality creates a negative political perception, and a negative political perception is created by a negative political reality. Likewise, a positive political reality creates a positive political perception, and a positive political perception is created by a positive political reality. The threatening financial reality of the collapsing economy created its politically negative perception of the economy, and American citizens' political negative perception was created by the reality of a highly unstable economy. For example, the reality of the Iraq war changed the perception of how most Americans viewed the war, and this perception changed from very positive in 2003 to very negative by 2006. Negative perceptions can also produce positive realities. For example, the American public's perception of the war created new positive realities. The new positive reality was Barack Obama, the first Afro-American president, a forty-seven-year-old Illinois senator who had only a year and half of Washington experience, being elected president of the United States. Another positive reality was record numbers of Americans turning out to vote in a historic 2008 presidential election, and many young people, for the first time, voted and found their rightful place in the political process. A negative reality can also create a positive reality. The many negative political and financial problems that happened during the Bush administration created the Obama administration, an administration of hope, enthusiasm, optimism, and rationalism that will attempt to turn hard economic times into an age of equal and opportuned prosperity. It is doubtful, however very arguable, that had there not been an Iraq war, Barack Obama, who initially opposed the war, would not have become president of the United States.

During the 2008 presidential election, there was an extremely negative public perception of President George Bush, Vice President Dick Cheney, the Bush administration's policies, and the Republican Party. These negative public perceptions were worsened by the harsh reality of massive political problems such the collapsing U.S. and global economies, massive job losses, and a drastic and rapid deterioration of U.S. financial and political credibility around the world. This negative national public perception, along with the negative realties of national and international problems that were created during President Bush's term, were the bases of President Barack Obama election to the highest office in this nation. The negative perceptions and negative realities of many of the Bush administration's failed policies had become so great that it created a historic national and global celebration of the end of the Bush administration. On election night, November 4, 2008, the majority of Americans and the world celebrated the end of President Bush's eight-year term. Never before had so many Americans and the world been so glad and anxious to witness the end of the term of a U.S. president.

The damaged and negative image of the Republican Party, and loss of the presidential election, also emotionally sparked many people, even many Republicans, to call for a change in the Republican Party's political and social ideology and in their approach to solving national and international problems. Many Republicans blamed President Bush for ruining the image of the Republican Party. It is arguable to conclude that President Bush is the main cause of the tarnished Republican image and why Senator John McCain lost the 2008 presidential race. However, many Americans blame both President Bush and the Republicans for many of the nation's failures in the last eight years of the Bush administration. The negative public perception of the Republican Party convinced and motivated the majority of Americans to turn to a new leader, like Barack Obama, to help solve this country's many political and social problems and to transform this nation into one of the highest levels of governing, political and social intellectualism, and political and social enlightenment.

A national and international negative stigma and strong dislike for the Republican Party created the Obama political, social, and cultural phenomenon that has grounded a positive energy of change like we have never seen simultaneously in America and the world. Why is the argument for change so valid, timely, and relevant? Are the prolonged and seemingly endless wars in Afghanistan and Iraq the reason people want change? Was it those high gas prices during the spring and summer of 2008 that were a great financial burden to consumers, while the gas and oil companies racked in massive profits? This, with many other factors, fed this urgent need for political change. Was it the awareness to combat global warming and to transition to alternative energies, such as solar, wind power, and electric cars, that motivated and inspired people to search for that unique leader, Barack Obama, to lead this great nation to that higher political and social level? Did the lack of confidence in the Bush administration create this mass urgency for a new way of doing things in American politics? Had the public's perception that the government did not care about its ordinary citizens reach a boiling point and finally a tipping and turning point?

First, the argument for change can only be valid if there is a need for change. Second, the public must recognize the need for political and social change before any change can happen. Third, the leader, like Obama, must argue the validity of the change and make a plan that will create the political change that the public desires. After the Iowa caucuses, in which Barack won a decisive victory with his inspirational message of change, all the other presidential candidates, especially Hillary Clinton, jumped on the bandwagon of "bringing change" to America and to American politics. The other candidates finally recognized after Barack's big win in Iowa how much American citizens desperately believed that a change of political direction in our society was necessary. In the end, the American voters elected Barack Obama as the forty-fourth president, because he personified and embodied those great elements of political, economic, and social change.

This desire for change in the 2008 election was stronger than it had ever been in recent history, and this demand for drastic and rational change caused many American voters to abandon their traditional political parties, change their political philosophies and ideas, and accept a new and higher way of political thinking and new political leadership in Washington. The year 2009 is not going to be just a year of change of the political parties in Washington from the Bush administration to the Obama administration, but it is going to be a mental, emotional, and spiritual change of American citizens' political and social intellect and enthusiasm that will be fully manifested in our political process.

During the primaries, the other presidential candidates futilely tried to steal Barack's arguments for political change, because it was an easy case to make at that economically troublesome time in our country. Even in the general election, Senator John McCain unsuccessfully tried to steal the change argument, because he and his campaign saw that the American public had reach a point where change was not a option but a national and international necessity this nation and the world felt was long overdue. While Barack was going around the country preaching and arguing his case for change, he did not have to lie to the American public about the greatly needed changes in our political, social, economic, and health-care system. These problems already and clearly necessitated changes, and the majority of Americans deeply felt and perceived that changes were necessary in all these and more specific areas at this critical time in our history.

Barack was not only arguing that change was urgently and desperately needed in our political system, but also that he was change and change was him. Arguing that he was a personification of change was the greatest argument that Barack could make, because if he is change and the country is demanding change, he is the leader that American citizens should vote into the White House. That is what happened on November 4, 2008. The American people decided that his argument for change was more than valid and that he was that embodiment of the kind of political change that would positively transform this great nation into a greater nation.

The public's demand for change was not only for structured and physical changes in government, in Washington politics, and the entire political system. American citizens also wanted a change in the energy and dynamics of its leaders. We Americans wanted to see a more inspiring and motivating leader in the White House and were looking for a more upbeat energy than we felt from the Bush administration. We, American citizens, have transcended to a level of political awareness where we realized that the U.S. president should not just have the political skill to solve problems but should also have an aura and energy that can intellectually and emotionally connect with the nation and the world. Barack, more than any of the other presidential candidates, had the intellectual and emotional connection that had not only grounded a national hope and a national optimism but also had the potential to create and ground a world peace, global respect, and international credibility for our great United States of America.

One of Barack's biggest arguments for change was the foreign policy argument to create a high-level diplomatic dialogue with our enemies. Barack's argument of sitting down and talking to our enemies was valid, rational, and sound, because he understood that continuing the Bush administration's foreign policy of not directly talking to our enemies until all conditions were met had not worked and had deteriorated U.S. diplomatic efforts around the world. Barack argued that countries should not have to agree with the United States and meet all of our conditions before we have direct talks with them. He had learned these great diplomatic lessons of having direct talks from former president Reagan and former Soviet president Mikhail Gorbachev. At first, Reagan and Gorbachev refused to have direct talks with each other. Instead, they spoke negative rhetoric and harsh political criticism of each other. Finally, in the mid-1980s, Reagan's diplomatic advisers convinced him that direct talks were essential for any chance of Russian-U.S. diplomacy, and Gorbachev agreed. After the United States and Russia started direct talks, President Reagan and President Gorbachev became more trustful and comfortable with each other and eventually became very good friends. Almost overnight, a false and old wall of fear and distrust between the two superpowers crumbled after many decades. However, approximately twenty-five years later, in the summer of 2008, during Russia's short-term invasion of Georgia, U.S.-Russian relations had turned for the worst. It had already gone sour with the Bush administration's nonnegotiable decision to install a missile defense system in Europe, which Russia considered to be a threat to their national security. Like Reagan and Gorbachev did in the mid-1980s, President Obama and Russian president Medevev must sit side by side, directly talk about U.S. and Russian problems, and try to compromise rationally and fairly. This can only happen when both leaders transcend foolish, silly, personal and national pride, fear, stubbornness, and narrowmindedness. When that happens, the heaven of political diplomacy can ground between both nations like a political salvation and blessing that make enemies into friends, the negative into the positive, war into peace, and sadness into joy. President Obama is a full embodiment of this kind of higher diplomacy.

Barack intellectually and emotionally understood that opening direct talks with enemies is not only to reach agreements but to immediately ease political and emotional tensions between nations. Barack knows that there are great psychological lessons and benefits to talking directly with adversaries. Trust can begin to be built, and nations can get a sense of what the other one wants. Obama clearly understood that directly talking to your enemy is much safer than not talking with your enemy, because with direct communications, one knows what one's enemy is thinking. It is better to know what your enemies are thinking than not to know what they are thinking, doing, or planning. Barack's high-level diplomatic thinking and philosophy can prevent wars and allow opposing nations to do very pragmatic things, such as trade with each other and open up other forms of business with each other. Barack understood that direct talks may not produce results overnight, but that diplomacy is a process that requires patience and a mutual respect between opposing nations. President Obama, with his new Secretary of State, Hillary Clinton, has a great opportunity to transcend this country and the world to one of the highest levels of diplomacy and peace. More than any other domestic or international policy, this argument for a changing to a more effective diplomacy to create world peace and better U.S. relations with the world will be a great part of President Barack Obama's legacy. This is definitely a change from the Bush administration's policy of not talking to our enemies, which has only alienated them more and caused countries such as North Korea and Iran to strongly pursue the creation of nuclear weapons and a country like Venezuela to become more emotionally and verbally hostile toward the United States. Barack argued during the campaign that it is in the best interest of the United States to exhaust fully all diplomatic efforts before using military force against any nation, because this is the logical and sound-minded change that our nation and the world desires and needs.

During the presidential campaign, there was also that silent argument for change that Barack Obama embodied as he traveled across the country. This argument was not written in speeches, or heard or seen on television, radio, or the Internet. Even though this argument was not articulated in words, the American people silently heard, felt, and understood it. This silent argument baffled the other presidential candidates during the campaign. It confused and stunned Hillary Clinton and her campaign in the primary elections, causing her to switch her political strategy and start using Barack's theme and arguments for change in the New Hampshire primary. This dynamic and silent argument is still strongly embraced and welcomed around the world. It is a special something that one must innately have. One cannot pretend and act like one has it. One must have it. During the presidential campaign and 2008 presidential election, the American people knew which presidential candidate possessed and personified this silent argument for change. Barack Obama, the forty-fourth president of the United States, was and is the silent argument of change, and he personifies and is the politically and social incarnation and reincarnation of this argument for changing the way politics is done in America. He looks like change. He acts like change. He talks and walks like change. He naturally possesses the aura of change, the levels of change, and the dynamics that can create change. The years 2009 through 2012 will need no words to persuade for change, because they are and will be the grounding and the full manifestation of a political divinity and a new political and social enlightenment in a nation that now has a leader, Barack Obama, to transcend it and its great citizens to a higher political and social plane and a higher political and social consciousness.

—Chapter 8—
What an Obama Presidency Means to the Advancement of Black People

(The fullest manifestation of Martin Luther King Jr.'s "I have a dream" speech)

As a black American, I can write this chapter with the highest level of truthfulness, appreciation, and sincerity, and I can honestly give a fair and correct assessment of what a Barack presidency would mean to every past, present, and future black American and how it will positively affect and impact the black community in America. Even though two former presidential candidates, the Reverend Jesse Jackson and the Reverend Al Sharpton, were black, Barack Obama is the first black candidate with a legitimate and high chance of winning the Democratic nomination and winning the presidential election in November 2008. Jesse Jackson did come in a strong second place for the Democratic nomination in 1988. Jesse Jackson, however, lacked something that Barack Obama had. That was the ability and dynamics to transcend white America and convince them to vote him into the White House. To Jesse Jackson's credit, he did have a great white following, though not like Barack's; however, there was still a national sense in the Democratic Party and in the nation that he was not electable by white America and that the country was not ready to elect a black president. Barack Obama was a different story, a much different and higher political level who had demonstrated that he had as much a chance, if not a better chance, of being elected president.

Barack becoming president of the United States of America would be the grounding and full creation of Martin Luther King Jr.'s "I have a dream" speech, and he is a full embodiment and personification of King's dream. Barack's success as a presidential candidate made 2008 a year of history, celebration, thankfulness, and praise for black people. A year of rejoicing and remembrance of a dark, long, American history of slavery, discrimination, hatred, and a vicious racism that was triumphed over with the historical moment and political success of Barack Obama as the new U.S. president.

Barack Obama's political success as an Afro-American, which was long overdue, seemed to have surprised the black community as much or even more than it did the white people and other races. This is mainly because blacks did not feel that a black person, no matter how qualified, experienced and intelligent, would be elected by white America, at least in their lifetime. Barack proved to black America that it could be done by doing it. As Barack continued to win primaries and successfully move through the campaign, more blacks gained confidence in Barack and started believing that he could win the Democratic nomination and the presidency.

This confidence in Barack is significant to the black community, because confidence in his success is inseparable from the progress and success of black people across the country. A Barack presidency will inspire and motivate many blacks to fulfill their American dreams and let them know and see that many racial barriers have been torn down. Barack, who has become the political savior for our entire nation, is the black American savior, because he is the personification of the solutions and answers to black people's problems in America. Barack is the physical, mental, and emotional embodiment of transcending anger of slavery, transcending past and present racism, transcending low self-esteem and lack of self-love, and transcending lack of self-respect and an endless cycle of self-victimization.

It has always been this self-victimization that has caused black people to feel inferior to each other, to other races, and to feel they are and were always treated unfairly by other races, especially by white people. Barack is the transcending of racial victimization. This is a great example and great pathway to a better life in America for all Afro-Americans. That is, to understand and learn to take full responsibility for their actions and stop blaming white people for every problem that is plaguing and destroying their black community. Barack Obama has learned these lessons of self-victimization and self-responsibility, and black people must do the same, because transcending self-victimization automatically creates self-responsibility. For example, when one stops viewing oneself as a victim of everyone and every circumstance, one can clearly see what is happening around oneself and take full responsibility and actions to improve oneself and one's community.

Barack is a great example of self-security and self-confidence. He is not trying to be white; nor is he trying to act like a certain kind of black person. He is confident in his own skin and feels good about who is as a person. When black America embraces this kind of high self-confidence and self-security, it will no longer consciously or unconsciously feel racially inferior about itself or anger at whites for their racist past.

Self-victimization is black people's worst enemy. Even though this feeling of being a victim to the white race is a result of a long, dark history of black slavery and discrimination, this is no excuse to be a victim. Being a victim is calling oneself a loser and a nobody. When one accepts that one is a victim, it causes one to give up. A victim has no hope or strength, because nothing is worth fighting for or achieving. Some blacks think that being an angry victim of racism and blaming white people for anything that hurts the black community is standing against racism. That is not true. It is the opposite. Standing against racism is totally different than becoming a victim of racism. Martin Luther King Jr. peacefully, firmly, and courageously stood up against racism while not falling victim to racism and racist white America. Not being a victim of any racist or any person is the true way to fight racism and to build and preserve your self-respect, high self-esteem, and pride. Barack is a great example of this. For example, when he was debating the other presidential candidates on national television, he did not feel inferior to them. He felt that he was just as intelligent, efficient, and politically skillful as they were. Barack represents the ending of black victimization and the beginning of black self-love, black hope, and a new black optimism for black Americans in America.

There are two kinds of self-victimization. First, there is the person who feels that he or she is helpless against someone or a political or social system. The second kind is when a person systematically blames another person, persons, or a political or social system for his or her problems. Most blacks fall into one of these categories. The first form of victimization is based on fear of oneself, others, and the political or social system. For example, a black person's fear of getting a better job and moving out of the ghetto is a victimization that keeps many blacks in our nation in poverty. A poverty that is more based on a negative and inferior state of mind than actual physical and financial causes. A change from an inferiorating state of mind to a positive state of mind will create and result in a better financial and physical environment.

The second form is rooted in anger toward oneself, others, society, and a political system. An example of this would be the Rodney King riots. After the severe police beating of Rodney King, blacks in Los Angeles and around the country felt they were victims of the an unfair justice system and that victimization produced much anger. Barack has overcome both of these types of self-victimization, because he knows that once he becomes a victim of another person, circumstance, or problem, he will fail, lose the fight, and never have the faith, self-confidence, and courage to achieve the success that he desires.

Self-victimization can be manifested physically and mentally. When black people were slaves, they were physical victims of slavery. Things such as lynching of blacks by the KKK and many racist whites throughout this country's history also made black people physical victims. With the exception of the hate crimes that are committed against blacks each year, most blacks are no longer physical victims of racism. They are mental victims to racism or a victim to negative racial perceptions about them. Being a victim to racism or the perception of racism is very detrimental to any person, race, or society. There is still much racism, especially on a subtle level, in our nation. However, blacks must not allow themselves to become caught up in the ignorance of their racism or white racism and understand that high self-esteem, high self-respect, and a high love for oneself and one's race is the greatest cure for even the most racist of societies. Like Obama, blacks need to remember and realize that when racism is directed toward them, they do not have to become a mental slave and mental victim to such racial foolishness. Like Barack Obama and Martin Luther King Jr., they can overcome all odds, rise to the occasion, conquer this irrational racism, and reach the highest level of success.

The worst kind of mental victimization is when blacks perceive that every problem they have is white people's fault. There are black people who blame white people for everything. They can only see through the eyes of anger and emotional attachment to white people's past and present racism. These blacks' entire perception is that white people are their enemies and that white people, because of their racist past, should be held responsible for black people's problems. White America of the past did do an unbelievably inhumane thing to blacks, and even though the country has racially come a long way, there is still much racism today. However, that does not mean that black people should not take responsibility for their own problems and become mental slaves to racism. Barack has transcended all these things, and hopefully, all blacks will see him as proven example and a manifestation of a dream come true. Barack is a political and social flower that was able to bloom out of the racist thorns of the past.

Barack has instantly changed the image and negative stereotyping of black people. White America and all non-Afro-American citizens who have negative perceptions of black people will be able to free themselves of these negative images and fears as they watch Barack Obama, whose image is the image of greatness, a new level of political intellectualism, and a black American who loves and has a high self-esteem and self-respect for himself. There is good and bad in all races. There are negative and positive people in all races; however, there is a tendency in this country, whether intentional or unintentional, for more of the negative than the positive to be portrayed of black people in the news media. Barack Obama, as the president of the United States, allowed the other races and the black race to see the positive side of black people and to see the great achievements of a black person, which is many times overlooked in this nation and in this nation's history.

National awareness of black people's achievements, like those of Barack Obama and many other blacks, will decrease much racism in this country, because racism is not just rooted in hatred; it is rooted also in disrespect for a race. When the other races daily and systematically see great blacks like Barack on the television, Internet, and newspaper and hear him on the radio, they will start to build a respect for black people and their achievements, and this respect for black people's achievements will eventually evolve into a high respect for black people.

A Barack presidency will inspire and motivate black Americans to love and appreciate themselves as black people and black Americans. Having a black American in the Oval Office and in the highest position in the land will give the black community a high level of confidence that they can achieve their dreams as black people and American citizens. Barack Obama, as the U.S. president, will bring a self-respect, a higher consciousness and awareness to the black community, and give a new glorious meaning to the definition of being a black American. Former president Bill Clinton said that Barack Obama's political success as a presidential candidate was a big fairy tale. Black and white Americans knew that this was far from true. The majority of the Americans were fully aware that this was not a fairy tale, but the total grounding of Martin Luther King Jr.'s dream, a dream in which Barack Obama was judged by his character and political abilities and talents, not by the color of his skin.

—Chapter 9—
The Oneness of Politics and Dynamics

(Barack's image alone can heal and restore
U.S. relations with the world)

Not since the days of President John F. Kennedy and his brother Robert F. Kennedy have we seen such an energetic, charismatic, dynamic, motivating, and inspiring leader like Barack Obama. He and his high-level ideas of change have swept the nation off its feet and transcended this country to a political level that it has not seen and felt in many years.

Barack brings into the political field an energy that many leaders and politicians do not have, which is the ability to integrate a motivating energy into politics that moves people to participate in our great political system. The Barack dynamics have brought new voters, especially young voters, into the political arena, and he has politically aroused many American citizens who, in the past, were apathetic and totally disinterested in government and our political system. Barack has motivated and inspired millions of young voters, who in record numbers, cast their vote for Barack and also campaigned for him. Many of the political experts believe that no leader or politician in recent American history, and maybe in all American history, has been able to move young America politically and socially to go the polls and vote like Barack Obama has been able to inspire and motivate.

Barack understands how dynamics, energy, and the spoken word can inspire and unite the American people around a common cause and common message. During the New Hampshire debates, Hillary Clinton said that the spoken word did not matter. Barack argued back by saying that what a leader says does matter, because a leader's words can inspire and move people to participate in the political process. Participation in the political process will give all American citizens a great excitement and optimism to make this nation a better place for themselves and their children. Leaders' actions alone can create changes in laws and policies, but it takes a leader's words to inspire, motivate, and unite people to create a massive political and social change in our nation's political system.

This nation and the American public are longing for a kind of politics that is filled with energy, hope, and optimism. The public is tired of the old, boring politics that has no life, no energy, and no inspiration. Barack Obama brings a new hope and a new liveliness to our nation's political system. A hope and liveliness that made 2008 one of the most exciting presidential election years in recent history.

The power of dynamics in politics is not be underestimated. That is the energy to move, the energy to change, the energy to inspire and motivate, and the energy to unite people or a nation. Politics without dynamics is like a human corpse without breath. It is like a balloon with no air. It is like a car that burns gas without gasoline. Barack brought a moving energy into the presidential campaign that fascinated the other candidates and caused most of them to copy his message of change. Barack impressed the political experts and analysts and caused many people—the American public, the presidential candidates, our politicians and leaders—to rethink how they look at politics in America.

Throughout this book, I have discussed and argued how Barack Obama's political aura and political energy will have a great and massive impact on the American public and the nation's political system. However, I would also like to discuss Barack Obama's impact on the world. For world peace and international diplomacy, a Barack Obama presidency is exactly what the doctor ordered. Like our nation was looking for a strong dynamic leader, the world was also looking for an inspiring and motivating leader who will heal our country's relations with the countries of the world.

Because of a massive resentment of U.S policy and a personal and public hate for President Bush and his administration by the international community, this is the perfect time for a charismatic, dynamic, highly understanding, and diplomatic president like Barack Obama to enter the international political arena. The Barack dynamics, the opposite of President Bush's, will consciously and unconsciously cause other countries to look favorably on this nation. Other countries will see Barack Obama's high political intellect and his high level of political and social consciousness that he brings into international politics. Like our nation, other countries respected and honored our election of a higher level of international thinking. This higher level of international thinking, higher level of diplomacy, and higher level of world peace is Barack Obama.

When dynamics and politics become one, it emotionally moves people and their leaders to create ideas that are beneficial to the nation. The Barack Obama candidacy created a new love and enthusiasm for politics that can be compared to an athlete motivating and inspiring sports fans. Barack has done for politics what Tiger Woods has done for the game of golf. When Tiger Woods won his first grand slam tournament, the Masters in 1997, he motivated and inspired many people who had never played golf, and some who did not even like golf, to not only start playing golf but to love it as well. Barack Obama, like Tiger Woods, has brought a dynamics and energy to politics that is unprecedented.

This dynamic and emotionally moving energy that Barack spread across the country was not to be taken lightly, because this inspiring energy made him not just a great presidential candidate but it helped him evolve into a national leader with millions of emotionally and politically fired-up followers and supporters. That was the biggest difference between Barack Obama and Hillary Clinton. Hillary had many followers and supporters, but they were supporting her mainly because they wanted her to be president. With Barack, it was an entirely different story. Because he had a higher level of political motivation and enthusiastic political energy, Barack not only had followers who worked hard to put him in the White House, they were a massive political and social movement that was unified around his message of change and bringing about a brighter and better America. This was and still is a grounded political movement of high rational political and social change that will live on for many years to come. This a phenomenal movement that is growing by the day and is igniting a political talk that is exciting people about today's politics. This political movement of change, which Barack was energetically leading, became a national phenomenon. This movement of change has been embraced by the majority of American citizens, and it shows no sign of slowing down. The country and this political and social movement have become one, centered around Barack's message of change.

Barack has raised the bar and the standard for what the president and any leader should be like. A president and any leader must be able to motivate the citizens and excite them about a common cause that will enhance a nation. The country is bored and has become numb to our leaders and president, because they lack that much-needed inspiring and motivating skill that John F. Kennedy, Robert F. Kennedy, and Martin Luther King Jr. possessed and could effectively and successfully convey to the American people.

This country was not seeking just a change in domestic and international policies but also in dynamics and change in energy. It is amazing that Hillary Clinton and the Clinton campaign had strongly argued that Barack Obama was inexperienced as a leader, yet Hillary did not understand nor did she have that dynamics and highly charged inspiring political energy that the country deeply and desperately desired and needed. Barack knows that a real and true leader must allow his or her political energy to be felt and received by the people. When people can feel a leader's energy, they will unite behind him or her like a mighty wind blowing over the ocean. This will create a political wave of change that will transform this country into a nation where everyone will feel that his or her participation in the political system is needed, appreciated, and is an accomplishment that creates happiness for us, American citizens.

Barack has done something that is totally unprecedented in politics. It is common in television. It is common in the entertainment industry. Barack has been able to arouse and excite the younger generation about politics and his message of change. Never before has such a large number of young people wanted to vote and participate in politics. Young people are as excited about Barack as they are about Hollywood celebrities and pop stars. Barack is the new political celebrity and superstar who has positively and inspiringly turned politics into something that young people want to be involved with and make a major historic political impact with their participation.

Barack, as president, has the potential to unify the world under this message of change for the better, because the United States is still considered the leader of the world. Barack, as the new U.S. president, has the opportunity to step up and lead the world with his inspiring leadership. Even though the president does not have to unite the world under a common message, Barack Obama is intelligent enough and has the dynamics and energy to do this. He may not just be what our country needs but also what the world needs. Barack will be the right remedy for solving many of our world problems, because he has the dynamics, political energy, and diplomatic skill to bring world leaders together to solve many of the major world problems.

The Barack dynamics is not just a national phenomenon, but also an international phenomenon and political sensation. This message of change is not just for our nation but will spread to the four corners of the earth, because like freedom, change is an energy that all people innately desire to experience when the time is right. Every human being wants to change his or her life for the better. Every nation innately wants to change to become a better and more politically, socially, economically, and technologically advanced nation. Barack's message of change will permeate through the world like a sweet-smelling fragrance, because all people love the smell of this precious gift of life, the energy of change.

—Chapter 10—
Barack and White America

(Never has any black person in politics been able to mentally, emotionally, and politically attract such a massive following from white America)

In the mid-1980s, when Michael Jackson was at the peak of his entertainment career and creating great albums such as *Thriller*, he achieved a status, even though it was in entertainment, that no other black man had achieved in American history. This greatness of Michael Jackson was greatly measured by an ability and dynamics to attract massive and unprecedented number of white people to his concerts and to buy his albums, videos, and other Jackson products. When Michael was a child superstar with the Jackson 5, the black community was the core of the group's record sales; however, it was the national and international sell of records to the white community and non Afro-Americans that escalated Michael Jackson's career and entertainment status to a level arguably like no other entertainer of any race had reached in the history of modern entertainment.

Blacks having much success and breaking most racial barriers in the entertainment and sports world is nothing new and has happened much faster than in the political world. The political world is lagging far behind in racial equality, and this is evident in the low number of black governors, state and national senators, representatives, and leaders in major positions in our government. This low political success of blacks elected to important political positions made the Obama presidency a gigantic leap and accomplishment for black Americans, and it shattered and destroyed many racial barriers that existed in our political system.

Barack is doing in politics what Michael Jackson did in entertainment in the early and mid-1980s. He, like Michael Jackson, has crossed politically racial lines like no other person in American political history. The Reverend Jesse Jackson had much success in crossing racial lines in his 1988 presidential campaign, but nothing like Barack Obama had done. Like Michael Jackson did in entertainment, Obama did in the political arena, convincing millions upon millions of white people to fall in love with his political dynamics and energy. Barack's romance with white America was a political wedding that has been long overdue in this country, a country that has one of the darkest histories of racial injustice, racial inequality, and deeply rooted racial prejudices.

The best sign of Barack's expansive and massive appeal to white America was a flocking of white republicans to him and his political message of change and a better America. The Republican Party was more threatened by a Barack Obama Democratic nomination than a Hillary Clinton nomination because of his great liking among white Republican voters and massive white Independent voters. Barack's political and social attraction of white America was a phenomenon, because his high-level political dynamics triggered white America to rise mentally and emotionally above race and look at him as a black presidential candidate who should be treated and judged fairly and not based on the color of his skin. Barack has charismatically moved white America to listen to his message without any regard for his race. His inspiring words and high political and social intellect have impressed white Americans like no other black man in the politics of American history. There have been few black leaders, if any, who could move and inspire white America like Barack. Even Martin Luther King Jr., as great as he was, could not get white people to flock to him like they flocked to Barack Obama. Even though Martin Luther King Jr. had many white followers, there was too much racism in white America for him to achieve racially what Barack has been able to do. That is, to get white America to transcend racial hatred and prejudices in our nation's political system. However, because of so much racial hatred in the air in the 1950s and 1960s, Martin Luther

King Jr. could not come close to getting white America to transcend racial barriers. Instead, he had to settle for great civil rights achievements, passage of legislation through Congress, and desegregation rulings by the Supreme Court. Even after all these things were done, there was still too much anger, racism, and a great divide between black and white people in a country that loudly proclaimed to the world that it had learned the lessons of slavery, discrimination, equality, freedom, and justice for each of its citizens.

Barack is in a different time than Martin Luther King Jr. He is in a time when people are more racially tolerant and more willing to judge everyone individually and not as a race. Obviously, blacks today have more freedom than blacks did in the Martin Luther King Jr. era. White people decided to accept Barack Obama in politics the same way Michael Jordan was accepted in the basketball, Tiger Woods in golf, Michael Jackson in entertainment, and Muhammad Ali in boxing. Barack Obama has not only become the black people's political superstar, but he has become a political superstar, idol, and role model for white America as well.

White America's support of Barack Obama shows that it has started learning the lessons of its racially discriminating, prejudiced, and hateful past toward blacks. White America's vote for Barack Obama symbolizes a transcending of white people to a racial level where they accept racial equality and are willing to give a qualified black, like Obama, an equal chance to be president of the United States.

A Barack presidency will not only be a historic moment for black Americans, it will also be a historic moment for white American citizens, because white America will have fulfilled the part of Martin Luther King Jr.'s dream of black and whites equally holding hands in the political arena. Martin Luther King Jr. knew that white people's equal acceptance of blacks was as important as blacks' love and respect for themselves. King knew that white people's ability to transcend all racial barriers and hatred was as important as the civil rights and voting bills that were passed in the 1960s. Barack's political and social dynamics will positively impact the racial beliefs and racial perceptions of white citizens of our country as much as the black citizens.

Barack Obama has the high consciousness and aura that make white America forget about his race and listen to his message of change. Many black leaders in America have not been successful at convincing white people to listen to their political and social voice. Many failed to communicate to white America, because their message was too threatening or perceived to be too racially threatening to white people. However, Barack can naturally communicate to white America in a way that makes it want to unite with him and not fear or feel racially, politically, or socially threatened by his message. Barack's ability to unite white Americans behind his political energy and political aura is a historical phenomenon, a historic phenomenon that landed him in the White House. A historic phenomenon that shocked and took the Hillary Clinton campaign by surprise. Barack has excited whites at a level that we have not seen in politics since Robert Kennedy. White people love him and see a political and social greatness that is far beyond judging him by the color of his skin.

Barack and his relationship with white America will positively affect the race relations between white America and black America. White people's liking of Barack Obama will translate into a racial acceptance of black people, because Barack, as president, will help white people transcend many racial barriers, negative perceptions, and stereotypes that they have of black people. The respect that white people will have for Barack will be translated into respect for black people. White people will see in Barack Obama that positive side of black people, that highly intellectual side of black people, and that greatness and strength black people possess. When Barack Obama was elected president, white America saw the black community through Barack Obama. Barack Obama became the window and mirror of the black community. White America looked through this window and at this mirror and saw black America. This will be the Barack Obama black America, which is a higher-level black America that will be more economically, politically, socially, and intellectually advanced.

How black people view Barack Obama will also affect how white people view black people, because the black perception and liking of Obama will have a great influence on the political and social direction of the black community. Black people, like white people, saw Barack as a mirror of themselves. When they look at Barack, they see themselves, their communities, and want to advance to that level of social and political progress that Barack has achieved. When black people look through the mirror of the Barack energy, they will see a black person like themselves who has set a high standard and example for them to follow. When black communities pattern themselves after Barack's greatness, it will increase the self-love, self-responsibility, and the political and social consciousness of the black community that will take black people to a much higher level as American citizens.

As a result of a Barack presidency, this higher level of black America will become more respected by white America, and white people will finally see, fully respect, and accept the greatness of black people that for many years was suppressed, not recognized, and not fully credited in this country. Barack Obama, a biracial Afro-American, will be the median between black people and white people. His presidency will heal that negative perception and racial fear that whites have of the black community, and he will be the one who will finally join the hands of the two races and unite them in that brotherhood and racial love that Martin Luther King Jr. spoke of in his "I have a dream" speech. Barack will finally be able to do what Martin Luther King Jr. spoke and dreamed about, and that is, to break down that final racial barrier. That racial barrier is racial inequality that for many years made it impossible for a qualified black man to be nominated for and elected to the highest political position in this nation.

As Barack continued to run a successful and great campaign and looked like he could take the White House by storm and surprise, the Clinton campaign and the Republican presidential campaign realized that they had underestimated him. It is not just Barack Obama his campaign's opponents had underestimated, but his opponents underestimated the racial tolerance and open-mindedness of many white Americans. Whether they admit it or not, the Republican Party was hoping that white America would think twice about electing a black man as president; however, the Republican Party had been totally wrong about white America's feelings about electing this politically electrifying black leader and politician to the White House. During the campaign, the latest general election polls showed Barack leading Senator John McCain. This was a sure sign that white America had come a long ways since black slavery, the viciously suppressing years of Jim Crow, and the cvil rights struggle of the 1950s and 1960s. The Republican Party was hoping and praying that white America would turn its back on Barack and not vote for him because of his race. Because of being politically incorrect and also afraid of being embarrassed by any accusation of racism, the Republican Party will not dare speak publicly about such desires; however, this was the silent hope of the Republican Party. This was its only hope of defeating Barack Obama. A hope that seemed to fade away like the sunset into the ominous night sky.

If Barack becomes the next president of the United States, it may not only be him that is the hero, nor his campaign staff, but it will also be white America and white America's racial tolerance that will also be the heroes of the 2008 election. White America's willingness to elect a black president is and was as historic as electing a black president itself. White America's judgment of Barack by who he is and not by his skin color is as much a fulfillment of Martin Luther King Jr.'s dream as a black man sitting in the Oval Office of the White House. The racial dynamics of having Obama as president will motivate and inspire the black community, but it will also have transcended white America to a higher level of racial consciousness, racial awareness, and racial love.

—Chapter 11—
Americans Are Looking for a Political and Social Savior

(Barack carries the message of political and social salvation)

Throughout this book, I have discussed how Barack's political dynamics have captivated and influenced American citizens; however, there was more to his massive public appeal than his energy, dynamics, message of change, high political intellect, and high level of political awareness and consciousness. There was an emotional political ingredient that was making this presidential election more exciting and energetic than any presidential campaign in recent history. That was the public's yearning and desire for something big to happen in the political arena of our nation. American citizens were looking for someone to drop from the political heaven with political manna and feed them with this manna of political change, political know-how, national confidence, hope, and a national faith that could politically unify the country. The American public was looking for and was ready to embrace that political savior. American citizens want a political savior who can solve national and world problems and can change the course, not only of the country, but of world politics.

In recent history, the people of this nation have accepted and voted for leaders as if voting for them was just part of their duty as an American citizen, but 2008 is different. The voting public has raised the standard of what it takes to be president. Having much political experience, much political knowledge and political skill was not good enough for the American people. The American public was looking for that political and social savior. One who has the dynamics and an energy that could inspire the entire country to improve itself, to actively participate and be enthusiastically involved in our government. The American people were looking for someone rational and sound-minded, but also different, to step into the White House and help lead and transcend this nation into a new and better nation. The American people have not only claimed Barack Obama as their candidate of change, but they have gone even further to claim him as their national and international political and social savior.

None of the other presidential candidates, even with all their political experience, talents, and know-how, possessed the dynamics and energy that would make the American people look to him or her to be a political savior. Barack had a special aura and a political level that made the American people feel that he was the one who would totally change the dynamics, energy, and consciousness of our nation's politics.

When any society or nation is looking for and feels that it needs some kind of savior, whether it is in politics, religion, sports, or entertainment, this need for someone to intervene and save is usually determined by outer circumstances and problems that have made people desperate for someone to come and save the day. That is, save our nation's politics and government with a high level of political thinking and philosophy that will pour and spread a political salvation and political healing across this nation. Our nation had reached a state of desperation where people were frustrated with the war in Iraq, extremely high gas prices, an economic recession, a decreasing housing market, and many more domestic and international problems. When these problems reach a tipping point, the public searches for that special person to come and help solve these problems. Barack Obama was the one the majority of Americans felt would be able to help change the problems into solutions and change national frustration into national hope, confidence, and a brighter and happier tomorrow.

Barack's silent and humble claim to be the savior of U.S. politics and government, and the American public's acceptance of this claim, made his election and presidency one of the most historic presidential elections and potentially the most important presidential terms in our history. The phenomenon of Barack as the political savior of American politics cannot be legitimized by him alone; it must also be supported by the public. American citizens believed that Barack was that special someone from outside of the Washington politics, not just the typical politician and leader that is in Washington today. The American public has placed a special confidence and special hope in Barack's dynamics to turn this country around and into a much better country. This feeling of public confidence in a president's dynamics and ability to change has not been felt since the days of President John F. Kennedy. The president having confidence in the people, and the people having confidence in the president, is what creates a great nation filled with much optimism and a national enthusiasm, which makes American citizens participate in their political system.

When a nation or society reaches the point where it demands immediate changes in its political system, its political leaders, and its nation's political philosophies, it is usually the public, whether they realize it or not, that has created the message of the messenger. For example, Barack could not get the support for change if the public did not want change. Barack has filled the political void that the public wanted filled. That political void was to change a nation that the majority of Americans felt was politically and socially going in the wrong direction. Because of the frustration and lack of confidence with the Bush administration, the American public created the message and energy of change that Barack genuinely felt, embraced, and articulated back to the American people. This energetic relationship between leaders and their supporters has always happened. That is, a relationship where the citizens express their needs to their leaders and the leaders accept, listen to the needs of their citizens, and become their political voice. That was what happened in this nation. The American people have voiced concerns in the last three to four years about wanting a change of course, and Barack, while traveling around the country, heard these concerns and integrated them into his political rhetoric and message of change. This message of change that was spoken by Barack was articulated back to the people, which creates a massive political energy and political and social attraction between Barack and millions of American citizens. Bringing political and social change, a higher political and social level, a higher political and social consciousness and awareness was what Barack naturally brought to the table of politics. When his energy of change connected with the American people's desire for change, it created a dynamics that can transcend a nation to a political and social level never seen in our American history.

This oneness of Barack's leadership with the public's outcry for change and a higher level of politics in our nation was the beginning of a new era. It was the beginning of an era where a leader can inspire and motivate the public, and the public can inspire and motivate the leader. It takes this two-way political and social relationship between the public and a leader to bring about the positive and drastic changes that American citizens were demanding.

This high-level dynamics of the oneness of political leadership and political citizenship is the greatest and most phenomenal political level and political system that can be created. This is that high democracy that our forefathers dreamed about being created in this country. A creative democracy where the leader and the public feed on each other's energy and unify their visions for this great nation.

Barack suddenly appeared as the political savior, because there was a negative energy between our leaders and the American public. The distrust of, lack of confidence in, and frustration with the Bush administration and its policies had reached an all-time high for American citizens. During the last two years, Barack felt, empathized, sympathized, and carefully listened to these political frustrations and political fears and integrated his message of hope, optimism, faith, confidence, and political problem solving into the political and social needs of the public. When a leader meets the political and social needs of the public, the public feels a sense of political salvation. The public develops a great faith and confidence in the leader, the leader's decision making and policies, and this public's confidence is received by the leader, who sends this confidence, trust, and faith back to the public. This mutual trust and exchange of energy creates a country where everyone will feel a sense of national self-worthiness and national pride as an American citizen.

As Barack Obama and Hillary Clinton battled for the nomination, the public had a chance to witness a drastic contrast between those two candidates. Hillary said she had the experience to make necessary changes, but Barack had a much higher aura and consciousness of change that the public felt from him. Even though Hillary Clinton, if elected, would have been the first woman president, that would have been a drastic change as far as gender was concerned. However, the public felt and had a higher sense that a Barack presidency would bring a much higher political dynamics and a much higher level of change to today's seemingly ineffective politics. There was even a sense in the nation that Barack's energy, political enthusiasm, motivation, and inspiration would bring a greater change than the historic fact that he is the first Afro-American president.

In order to be a savior of anything, one must have the characteristics of and understand the role of a savior. First, a savior comes on the scene at the right time. Second, there must be a need or great problem or crisis that necessitates the need for a savior. Third, the public must have reached a high desperation and frustration level with the present crisis. Fourth, the public must be longing for a savior. Fifth, there must be a mass acceptance of the savior by the public. Sixth, the public must feel that no one else is capable, except the savior, of solving their problems. Seventh, the savior must be accepted by the public for him or her to be the savior. Eighth, the savior must be fully aware of his or her purpose and mission and be totally committed to achieving that mission. Barack Obama's ability to fulfill his mission, purpose, and commitment to changing the present level of politics to a higher level of politics, leadership, and governing characterizes him as a real political savior of American politics.

—Chapter 12—
Obama and the People of Power

(The people of power want a change)

Throughout this book, I have emphasized the American public's desire for change of political direction, its frustration with today's politics, and its yearning and demand for new national leadership. However, like American citizens, the people of power want change. The people of power whom I am speaking of are not rich Hollywood celebrities, powerful politicians, and somewhat wealthy Americans. I am referring to those unbelievably wealthy individuals who really run and control the national and global economy. These are big-time investors and bankers, mostly foreign, who have massive investments in this country. Many of these foreign investors are the Chinese, Japanese, and Saudi Arabians who have bought expensive Treasury notes and own many U.S. dollars. This country is in great debt to these investors.

Whether it was a loss of confidence in the Bush administration's economic and foreign policies or just an innate feeling of great unease about a U.S. economy that had slipped into a recession, the people of power seemed to be open to a change of leadership in our country. They, like American citizens, were looking for a president and a new administration that could come in and help stabilize an unstable U.S. economy that has caused world financial markets to destabilize. The people of power like political and financial stability, and things such as the prolonged war in Iraq and the tarnished U.S. image around the world has had a negative impact on the global economy and world markets and has created much anxiety, fear, and even frustration with the people of power.

The people of power were looking for a new face and new blood to lead the United States and the Western world and restore the U.S. image and reputation with the rest of the world. They know that improved U.S. relations with the rest of the world will help stabilize domestic financial markets and the global economy.

Like the American people, the people of power became attracted to this message of change that Barack Obama articulated. Normally, the people of power fear and are threatened by someone who wants to change the financial, political, or social status quo. However, they considered Barack Obama to be an exception. Unlike presidential candidate John Edwards, who seemed to have a polarizing and hostile attitude toward the business, corporate, and commerce community, the people in power felt that Barack Obama was economically intelligent enough to understand the importance of working with the national and international business and commerce community. Barack will implement policies that are helpful to the middle class and poor but will not hurt the rich investors. Even though Barack Obama genuinely argued that he will financially help the poor and middle-class Americans who support the economy from the bottom, which is consumer spending, the people in power feel that he will still support the rich investors who support the economy from the top by making big investments into the U.S. economy. The relationship between Barack Obama and the people of power may become a good business relationship, because Obama understands the economic connections between the rich and the poor. That connection is that the rich help the poor by creating the jobs and the products, and the poor helps the rich by buying the products of and working for small and large businesses.

Usually, the public and the people of power are not one or on the same political and economic page. The people of power usually want to go one way, while the public wants to go the other way. However, during the year 2008, the American public and the people of power were on the same page. Both the American public and the people of power agreed that the United States needed fresh, new leadership and a change of political direction in many of its domestic and foreign policies. Never before in recent history have the people of power been so dissatisfied, frustrated, and unconfident with U.S. leadership. The people of power felt that a Barack Obama presidency would be the exact opposite of a George Bush/Dick Cheney presidency. The people of power, like the American public, were willing to gamble on the young senator from Illinois, and it was a gamble that they, like American citizens, felt was worth the risk. The people of power felt that it was crucial that a drastic change of U.S. leadership happen in 2008.

There seems to be no direct or subtle sign that the people of power were trying to prevent a Barack presidency. They may be thinking that Barack's leadership in a global economy was just what the doctor ordered. Even the thought of having an Afro-American president lead the free world seemed not to bother the people of power.

The people of power, like American citizens, were looking to Barack to bring a new energy and dynamics to the global economy and to world politics. They were hoping that a Barack presidency would improve the tarnished international reputation that the Bush administration, its policies, and especially the war in Iraq had created throughout the world. The people of power will use Barack for their interest and to bring about the changes that they want, and Barack is going to use them to bring about the beneficial political and positive economic changes that he wants for the country and the world.

The people in power have no intention of stopping Barack's domestic and international policies, because they understand and like his politically new frontier image of change. They feel that Barack's vibrant political aura and dynamics will restore a positive image to the United States and improve the U.S. reputation around the world. An improved U.S. image internationally will positively affect trade agreements and many aspects of commerce with other nations. The people of power want Barack Obama to be liked and supported by American citizens and the world so that he can have the political power and credibility to implement the people of power's global political and economic plan, which is stabilizing relationships with countries, and preventing wars and international confrontations that destabilize world financial markets. Barack has no intention of politically fighting with the people in power, because he knows that he needs them to help him maintain great political and economic relations throughout the world and to continue to invest big money in this country's economy. Barack will intelligently find that perfect balance of fulfilling the interests of both the people in power and American citizens, which consist of mostly the upper-middle class, middle class, lower-middle class, and the poor.

The people of power want an American president they know will be good for the global economy, not just the U.S. economy, which consists of two-thirds of the global economy. The big investors of the world will be looking for Barack to lead a global economy that will continue to bring in more investors and to prevent this global economy from falling into a world economic recession. The people of power trust that Barack will create and maintain an economic policy that will benefit world financial markets.

A Barack presidency will be attractive to the wealthy investors of a global economy, because international peace and diplomacy are very important in this global economy. A world of war and lack of diplomacy totally destabilizes domestic and world financial markets. For example, the Iraq war totally destabilizes the oil market, causing the price of a barrel of oil to increase rapidly. The people of power were very disappointed in the Bush administration's lack of world diplomacy and the way they conducted and mismanaged the Iraq war. A world of peace and high-level diplomacy means a flowing international commerce, and the people of power felt that Barack Obama had the more diplomatic and less polarizing image of all the presidential candidates. Even though Hillary Clinton understood the global economy, the people of power felt that Barack had a more diplomatic image and energy and could bring about a much higher level of political and economical diplomacy and stability.

The people of power will not interfere with Barack's leadership if he allows the big world investors to freely invest in the U.S economy and allow the United States to invest freely in all world markets. Likewise, Barack will not interfere with the people of power if they do not allow their financial interest to jeopardize the U.S. economy, which would financially damage American citizens. However, there seems to be a mutual understanding between Barack and the people of power that both the wealthy investors of the U.S. economy and all American citizens should be financially protected.

The people of power will look to Barack Obama to lead the economic and political frontier of creating new sources of energy and new technologies and to represent the new era of innovation and creativity that is quickly unfolding in the twenty-first century.

Obama's influence with the people of power is as important as his influence with ordinary American citizens. His support of the people of power is as significant as his support of the poor and middle-class American. His popularity or unpopularity with the people of power can affect his presidency as much as his popularity or unpopularity with the American public. Barack knows the people at the top are as important as the people at the bottom. The rich and powerful will set the political and economical tone from the top, and the middle class and poor will set the political and economic tone from the bottom. Barack will have to create an intelligent political and financial plan that will simultaneously benefit both the rich and the poor. Barack knows that tax relief for the rich is as important as tax relief for the poor. Relieving the rich of taxes will encourage the people of power to invest in the U.S. global economy. Relieving poor and middle-class American citizens of taxes will encourage consumer spending at the bottom. Higher consumer spending will increase employment for the poor and middle class, because the small businesses and the big corporations can hire more employees when consumers spend money in their businesses. Most of these consumers are the poor, lower-middle class and middle class. When consumer spending is high, corporations and small businesses can lower the prices of their products for the consumer and raise wages for their employees. This political and economic skill of equally negotiating with the rich and the poor will prove to be a vital and important part of the Barack presidency.

The people of power are expecting Barack to keep the economy stimulated from the bottom so that they can continue to invest from the top. The people of power and Barack Obama will have a mutual relationship about how to improve the global economy. Both Obama and the people of power realize that poor citizens and middle class should not be hurt; they should progress and prosper while the rich and powerful prosper. The ability to strike this delicate balance is the main reason why the people of power chose Barack Obama for president. In a global economy of this magnitude (the United States makes up two-thirds of the world economy), this ability to help financially stimulate the poor and middle class is more important to the people of power, because any financial stagnation at the bottom will definitely affect the people at the top. Barack will make sure that this financial flow from top to bottom and bottom to top becomes one and beneficial to all. This will be part of Barack's message of change: a change for how the people in power thinks, a change for how the rich view the poor, a change for how the poor and middle class view the rich, and a total awareness of how important the rich and poor are to each other. Barack Obama will be the leader of this historic moment of change in our nation's basic view of how our economy works. This is the change that the people of power wanted to happen, and they knew that Barack Obama is the better one to help direct and orchestrate this political and economic change.

—Chapter 13—
Why the Democratic Party Should Nominate Barack Obama

(Barack represented a new Democratic Party)

Since the South Carolina primary, where both Bill Clinton and Hillary Clinton angered and alienated the black community in South Carolina and across the nation because of controversial racial remarks regarding Martin Luther King Jr. and Jesse Jackson, the Democratic Party, especially its superdelegates, had seriously been debating if Hillary Clinton was too polarizing of a political figure to defeat the Republican Party in the national presidential election. Even powerful Democratic leaders such as Senator Ted Kennedy, who was close friends with the Clintons, was angered by those seemingly racial comments by both Clintons. Soon after the South Carolina primary elections, he endorsed Barack Obama for president of the United States.

The Republican Party campaign strategists publicly said that it would be much easier to run and win against Hillary than Obama, because Hillary was more polarizing than Obama, who was naturally more likable than Hillary. Even though Barack Obama had become much more politically vulnerable than before because of the Reverend Wright controversy and other controversies he has had to deal with in his campaign, the Republicans still felt that Barack had a political and social mystique and dynamics that would be difficult for them to defeat in the general election. Hillary was also still hated by the Republican voters because of bad feelings that lingered from her husband's presidency in the 1990s, and most Republicans and many Independents and Democrats were very resistant about Bill Clinton coming back into the White House as the First Man. However, after overcoming the Reverend Wright controversy and scoring big wins in Indiana and North Carolina primaries, Barack convinced the superdelegates of the Democratic Party that he could withstand powerful political punches and could be the next president of the United States.

After the South Carolina primary, Barack not only gained a momentum from the voters but great momentum and massive support from within the Democratic Party. Barack's convincing win in the South Carolina primary gave a clearer picture to the superdelegates in the Democratic Party and to the voters about who, he or Hillary Clinton, was the most electable candidate for the 2008 election. Barack, unlike Hillary Clinton, showed that he could unite the Democratic Party and the country, and while the Clintons were subtly and sometimes directly making race an issue, he stayed above the race issue and helped transcend his supporters and the country to envision a much higher level of politics and government.

Both Bill and Hillary Clinton also angered many of the superdelegates in the Democratic Party because they were constantly making many false statements and blatant distortions of Barack's political record and his political arguments. These factors, along with many others, decreased Hillary Clinton's likeability and national electability among voters, called into question whether she should be the Democratic nominee, and greatly created doubt over whether she could win the presidential election against John McCain.

There are many more reasons why the Democratic Party nominated Barack Obama instead of Hillary. First, Barack was a much better representation of change. He looked like political change, talked like change, and politically and socially felt like change to the American public. His aura and dynamics were the energy of change. More important, the American people felt that of all the presidential candidates, Barack Obama was the one who was more genuine about creating change. Earlier in the presidential race, the other presidential candidates copied Barack's message of change after they saw how many millions of Americans were attracted to and inspired by it.

Second, Hillary Clinton did not have that natural political dynamics that Barack had shown and openly expressed across the country. Even with all of Hillary's political experience, political skills, and talents, she did not have the political energy and enthusiasm that Barack possessed, articulated, and communicated to the American people. Barack's political aura and political and high reasoning level were something that was part of his inner self. This political aura and inspiring and motivating energy totally baffled, confused, and left the entire Clinton campaign without answers about how to defeat Barack Obama.

Third, this 2008 presidential election was going to be about which candidate had the greatest political and social vision for the country. The American people did not just want an experienced president and policymaker. They also wanted someone who had big dreams and great visions for the country and could help American citizens make those dreams a reality. Hillary Clinton could have made a good president, but unlike Barack Obama, she was not a great visionary like Martin Luther King Jr., John F. Kennedy, and his brother Robert F. Kennedy. She was a practical lawmaker, who had proven she could get things done. However, Barack had proven that not only could he get things done, he could create a vision for the country and inspire us, the American people, to have faith in that vision so that it can become a grounded and physical reality in this land of great and possible ideas.

Fourth, Barack Obama arguably was a more genuine candidate, and the country was looking and longing for a leader who had the sincerity and genuineness, like Barack. He seemed to have more truth and realness to his candidacy and political arguments than Hillary Clinton, and Barack seemed to give a more truthful assessment of a problem, an issue, or a candidate. Seldom did Barack distort or not tell the truth when discussing or debating an issue. For example, even though Barack said that he disagreed with many of Reagan's policies, he confidently acknowledged and explained that former president Reagan was arguably a great president who transformed the country with an optimism and inspired a decade of unprecedented entrepreneurship and economic growth that had a great impact on the country. Hillary and Bill Clinton totally distorted Barack's words about Reagan by telling voters that

Barack was saying that the Democratic Party did not have good ideas and the Republican Party had all the great ideas. Barack was simply saying that during the Reagan presidency, the Republicans, whether one agreed with them or not, were constantly creating ideas about how they thought the country should be governed. This distortion by the Clintons of Barack's assessment of Reagan and the Republican Party of the 1980s made Hillary look like a dishonest and insincere candidate who would do and say almost anything to win.

The most important reason I thought the Democratic Party nominated Barack was because the public and our national politics were in need of a great visionary and vision for the country. American citizens have seen many presidents who were very experienced in politics and government, but what the country had not seen in at least fifty or more years was a great visionary president. A visionary president is a president who can articulate and lay out a great vision for the country, inspire and motivate the majority of Americans to get behind that vision, and more important, make sure that he or she, as well as the American public, stay committed to grounding that vision into a national reality.

The likability of each candidate was definitely a factor that the superdelegates considered when nominating the candidates. Many polls have shown that the public thought that Barack was more naturally likable while Hillary put on an artificial personal front in order to be liked. Barack did not have to try to be liked; however, Hillary worked to make her image likable and favorable to the public. Barack could be himself, and the public liked and felt his sincerity, not the orchestrated, staged personality that it seemed Hillary publicly portrayed. Many voters expressed that Hillary had more of a look of anger than happiness and political optimism and that her mostly self-proclaimed strength and strong commander in chief image were more rooted in anger than in the strength of pure leadership. Anger and strength are not the same, even though sometimes people think that anger is strength. Anger is simply an expression of conscious or unconscious frustration, and strength is a confidence in oneself as a leader. Barack exemplified the characteristics of a pure leader. A pure leader, whose strength was rooted in leadership, high intellectual political principles, and great political ideas and visions for the country.

The Democratic Party increased its chances of winning and defeating the Republican machine in the November election by nominating Obama, because the Republican Party felt that it was much more difficult to run against an Afro-American candidate than Hillary Clinton. Even though Barack took some very tough political punches during the Reverend Wright controversy and when he made the controversial remarks about small-town America at a private fund-raiser in San Francisco, he still emerged as a stronger candidate after a convincing win in the North Carolina primary. The Republican strategy of politically wounding and bloodying Barack had failed. Barack survived his biggest political attack as a Democratic candidate and politically rose to his feet with a wave of superdelegate endorsements and with his greatest Democratic rival, Hillary Clinton, barely surviving politically. The fact that the Republican Party feared running against Barack Obama, and that it knew it might not be able to stop him from being elected president, gave strong reasons for the superdelegates to choose him as the Democratic nominee.

There were more reasons than just the Afro-American factor why the Republican Party did not want Barack, but Hillary, to be the Democratic nominee. This was the year that most Americans wanted political and social change. Barack, much more than Hillary Clinton, was a total contrast to the Republican nominee, Senator John McCain. This proved to be severely damaging to the Republican Party that fall, because the majority of the Republican voters wanted change as well. If Barack faced a Republican candidate in the national election, it could possibly be a landslide election, because some polls showed that Barack could possibly pull 10 percent to 20 percent of the Republican vote. This great potential to have a landslide election was another important reason for the Democratic Party to nominate Barack Obama to run in the general presidential election.

In addition to Barack attracting Republican voters, his nomination, unlike Hillary Clinton's, secured many of the Independent voters in the country. During the primaries, Barack totally crushed Hillary in the category of the Independent voters. It would have been to risky for the Democratic Party to nominate Hillary Clinton to run for president, because it would have lost 50 percent or more of the Independent voters to the Republican Party in the fall. Either party could not afford to lose too many of the Independent voters, because they would have great voice in determining the next president.

Because Hillary Clinton and Bill Clinton angered many blacks in South Carolina and across the country during the South Carolina primary after making a few arguably racial statements, a Hillary Clinton nomination would have angered blacks more and caused them not to vote or support the Democratic Party that presidential election, or even totally leave the Democratic Party. Many blacks probably would not have voted, because they no longer admired Hillary and Bill as they had in the past. Blacks would have seen the Democratic Party's rejection of Barack as the Democratic nominee as a sign that racism still heavily existed in America and in American politics. A seemingly perceived unfair rejection of an Obama nomination for president would have reminded blacks of the difficulty of a black man becoming president in America. The great political success of Obama had given blacks in this country a hope and an optimism that they could achieve equally to white people. A rejection of Barack by the Democratic Party, or putting him on the Democratic ticket as a vice presidential nominee, would not have been accepted by black people. I doubt that the majority of blacks would have voted Republican, but I do feel that many blacks across the country would have lost confidence in the Democratic Party. This is a sensitive racial issue that the superdelegates had to consider seriously before rejecting Obama, who had all the necessary delegates to win the Democratic nomination.

Finally, Barack, who would be the first Afro-American president, and Hillary, who would be the first female president, would make momentous history if either were elected president. However, even though a woman had never been president, it would be more historic and drastic of change for an Afro-American to become president. This is arguable and was argued all across the country during the campaign, especially by feminist groups, who felt that a Hillary Clinton presidency would be just as great as a Barack presidency.

A Barack presidency will be a more drastic change and greater history because of the vicious racial hatred, discrimination, and extreme prejudices that black people experienced for hundreds of years in this nation. Even though women experienced a form of suppression from men, whether it was subtle or direct, men's suppression of women in the past cannot come close in comparison to the most racially violent, degrading, and inhumane actions done to Afro-Americans in the past. That is, white America enslaved black people, lynched black people, and created and perpetrated one of the worst forms of racial discrimination in not just U.S history, but arguably world history.

One will be much better off being a woman in this country than being a black person. This is true of the far and recent past. For example, until the late 1950s, a black man, even if he were a rich, prominent black man, had to sit at the back of the bus, and a white woman, even if she were a poor, homeless white woman, could legally ask a rich black man to move from a front seat to the backseat. As much as women feel that they were abused and suppressed by men throughout history, and they were, there is no comparison with how women were treated and how black people were treated. For example, if Barack Obama and Hillary Clinton took a time machine into the past approximately 200 to 300 years, Barack would be a black slave, even if he were biracial like he is now. Hillary would probably be a prominent slave owner's wife, or she could be a slave owner herself. She would be the master and Barack would be the slave. Barack, as a slave, would have to obey Hillary's every command or he would be severely beaten or suffer a brutal death as a message to other slaves who might think about being disobedient to Hillary. As harsh as this argument and example may sound, this is the reality of how dark this country's racial past is and how divine a Barack Obama presidency is to the country. I could use thousands of more examples, some almost unbearable to mention, of how blacks were brutally and viciously treated throughout this country's dark and sour racial history.

One may think that this imaginary example of Hillary and Barack going back to those bad racial times is far-fetched. However, it is not. Unfortunately, that is the way it was and that is why as drastic and as great of a change as it would be for a woman, like Hillary Clinton, to be president, it will be much greater for an Afro-American, like Barack Obama, to be the president in a country where so many blacks shed their precious blood and sacrificed their lives so that black Americans today can be free and, like Barack Obama, run for the highest office in the land.

—Chapter 14—
Barack vs. the Republican Party

(Can the Republican Party stop Barack?)

This was the big and magical question that the superdelegates of the Democratic Party patiently considered when they chose to nominate Barack Obama, instead of Hillary Clinton, as the Democratic nominee. The Republican Party had always felt that it would rather run against Hillary than Barack. The Republicans knew that Barack, the first Afro-American Democratic nominee, would be more difficult to run against, because competing against a black presidential candidate in the general election would be a first for the Republican Party. There was no past general presidential election that the Republicans could study and be certain that it could defeat the dynamic and politically and socially inspiring Barack Obama. This was a new political terrain not just for the Republican Party but also for the entire nation. An election where this young, inspiring, black American, a full personification and symbolic embodiment of the American dream, impressively shocked the nation and the world with his highly unique intelligence and deep grasp of political and social issues when he debated his rival, Senator John McCain, in the three presidential debates. However, even the Republicans were finally surprisingly impressed with his ability to raise record-breaking amounts campaign money and bring in unheard of numbers of new voters, especially young voters, and finally created an electoral landslide.

The most frustrating and confusing thing for the Republican Party was how and why so many prominent, credible, and experienced political leaders endorsed and blessed this young leader as the best one to lead our great nation. The best example of this was when former secretary of state Colin Powell publicly endorsed Barack Obama three weeks before the presidential election. This powerful and timely endorsement was a nightmare and a half for the Republicans, because even though they had expected Powell's endorsement, they did not anticipate Powell to argue so strongly and effectively why Barack Obama was a much more skilled, intelligent, and inspiring leader than John McCain. What made this endorsement of Barack Obama much more significant than other endorsements during this and other presidential elections, was that Colin Powell did not just endorse Barack Obama's candidacy. He confidently substantiated that Barack would not just be a good and great president but be a president who would transform and electrify the nation and the world. Powell's endorsement was a tremendous political blow to the McCain campaign, not just because he was and is well-respected by Republicans and most Democrats, but because he endorsed and introduced the beginning of a new era and the ending of an old era. A new era in which Colin Powell said that Barack Obama would be better to lead our great nation into the next generation than John McCain. Colin Powell's endorsement was even more damaging to the Republican Party, and especially to John McCain's campaign, because he said the Republican Party had become very narrow-minded and was starting to show negative racial tones that were disturbing and embarrassing to him as a Republican. Colin Powell's endorsement was a stern, fair, and rational warning to the Republican Party that it was becoming politically and socially irrelevant to the American public. Powell's endorsement of a new era and a new generation, which he said would be better led by Barack Obama than John McCain, was also an endorsement of the ending of the Republican era and the beginning of a new Democratic Party that will govern from a new and higher level of politics and political philosophy. Colin Powell further shut and locked the door of the old Republican era by directly and honestly admitting that vice presidential nominee Sarah Palin was not qualified to be president of the United States and that her political and social narrow-mindedness had taken the Republican Party further right and in the wrong direction. Powell's argument about Sarah

Palin creating a more right-winged Republican Party was significant, because Sarah Palin, who had energized the Republican Party, could possibly run against Barack in 2012. Even though she energized the Republican Party, she was not politically or socially liked by Independent voters or swing voters, and she energized the Democrats to come out and vote against her and Senator John McCain on Election Day.

The Republican Party's fear of running against Barack was much more than him being an Afro-American candidate; there were many reasons why the Republican machine feared Barack Obama in the presidential election. First, Barack had a much more diverse national following than Republican presidential candidate, Senator John Mc"Cain. Barack proved this in the primary elections by winning many states that were both liberal and conservative. Barack's broad appeal to voters was a big political threat to the Republican Party, because unlike any other presidential candidate that we have ever seen, Barack had motivated more American citizens to register to vote. These newly registered voters, mostly young voters, had massively increased the Democratic base, which was what was so frightening to the Republican Party on Election Day, because these newly registered voters were not shown in the daily tracking polls. Most polls were based on voters who had voted at least once or twice. Both the Republican and Democratic parties knew that the election would possibly be determined by the number of new voters who were passionate enough to come out and vote.

Even though John McCain was a more moderate conservative than President Bush, his appeal to voters was not nearly as expansive as Barack Obama's national appeal. The thought that these newly registered Democratic voters would show up on Election Day in mass numbers was a political nightmare that the Republican Party hoped would not happen. If the Republican Party could not stop Obama's energizing appeal to the new voters, the Republican Party knew it would suffer a massive defeat on Election Day.

Second, the most frightening thing to Republicans was that a Barack presidency would represent the end of a nationally dominating and influential conservative movement that started with Barry Goldwater in 1964 and gained even more prominence during the Reagan presidency in the 1980s.

Barack Obama was the beginning of not a liberal movement but a political transcending and political enlightening movement. President Bush said in a news conference that the "stakes are high" for the Republican Party in the fall election. President Bush knew that an Obama win would end the political momentum of the conservative movement and politically ignite a new movement of change, enlightenment, and political and social advancement and progression that this country has never seen.

An Obama victory made the conservative movement look and feel like a minority and a powerless movement among a new, inspiring, and creative national movement of political and social change and a creative and fair way of governing this great nation. A Barack presidency increased the momentum of the movement for political and social change and motivated many Americans to help bring about a new politics in this nation. It even motivated many conservatives to transcend to this higher level of governing, political philosophy and thinking, higher political awareness, and political enlightenment. It was very difficult for conservatives to argue against Barack's rhetoric of transcending the regular old politics and bringing a higher level of politics to Washington. It was almost impossible for conservatives to convince the American people, and even some of the conservatives in their own party, that Barack's message of change was not the right message and not the right time for this nation to transcend to a higher level of governing.

Barack was a serious threat to the dominance and strength of Republican philosophy, especially the so-called old Republican establishment, because he attracted those liberal and moderate Republicans who wanted a change in the Republican policies in the nation's domestic and foreign issues. What terrified the Republican Party were those liberal Republicans who were open-minded enough to vote for a qualified black man for president. The worst scenario was that those Republicans who voted for Barack would permanently desert the Republican Party and become either a Democrat or independent voter. This became a real possibility if those more liberal Republicans sensed that John McCain's policies were too close to George Bush's policies. George Bush's unpopularity with some Republican voters made it easier for Barack Obama to come in and steal some of those Republican votes.

This threat of attracting so many Republicans to Barack's message of change would be the biggest problem for the Republicans, because like the Democratic voters, most of the Republican voters were looking for a drastic change in the political direction of the country. Barack, unlike John McCain, was a personification and representation of change. John McCain had very close ideas to those of President Bush, whose great unpopularity did not help McCain and the Republican Party win the presidential election. Even though John McCain surprised the nation by choosing as his running mate the first Republican female vice-presidential nominee, Sarah Palin, it was still difficult for John McCain to stand on stage with Obama and argue that he and the Republican Party had supported maintaining the political and social status quo. Barack was serious about making drastic changes from the many economic and national problems that were created while the Republican Party was in power. It would be extremely difficult for McCain to argue change when he supported the Iraq war and the majority of American people no longer thought the Iraq war was worth fighting. This argument and rhetoric of change that Barack articulated would not just be a powerful dynamics for Barack's campaign, but it would be a weapon that could pierce the very depth of the Republican Party, causing it and its ideas to be rejected and demonized by most Americans and labeled as the party that was totally out of sync and out of touch with present-day America. A Republican Party that is many light-years behind the new, high-level politics and governing that Barack has brought to the political table.

Another big worry for the Republican Party was that its conservative platform would not be good enough to stand up against Barack's message of a new America and a better America. When matched against Barack's message, the Republicans risked losing the confidence and trust of many Republican voters that came into the party during the Reagan years. Some of these voters had reached a stage of boredom combined with frustration with their own party. The Republican Party was afraid that Barack would paint them as the stagnated party, the stubborn and narrow-minded party that has principles, but not the correct principles to lead this country. The Republican Party knew that it would be easier for Barack, than Hillary, to make it look like the party of the old establishment and as preserving the old status quo and not the party of change. Barack, unlike Hillary, was not part of the old Washington political establishment.

Barack versus a Republican candidate in the 2008 election might consciously and unconsciously have shown a negative racial image on the Republican Party, because it was the Democratic Party that had gotten the credit for nominating the first black American for president. I use the word unconscious, because even if neither party mentions this historic nomination of a Afro-American for the Democratic nomination and this historic presidency, the fact was and is that the nation knows and is aware that it was the Democratic Party that was able to take the first major step in transcending race and give Barack Obama a fair chance to win the presidency. A Barack Democratic nomination reminded many voters in this election that the Republican Party was still that party that wanted to preserve the status quo and still has many politically and socially racial barriers to overcome. As the American public looked at Barack Obama as the Democratic nominee, they still saw a Republican Party that was not close to nominating a black man for president. A party that in the recent past has, and is still, making a big political mistake in not reaching out to blacks at the level that it should. Barack versus Senator John McCain was really Barack versus the Republican Party. When Barack defeated the Republican presidential candidate, Senator John McCain, that was not just a defeat of John McCain but a major defeat of the old racial ways of the conservative movement and Republican Party. A political party whose ideas are starting to become extinct, like the dinosaurs.

After Barack won twelve states in the Super Tuesday primaries that were held around the country on February 5, 2008, this convinced the Republican Party even more that running against Barack would be very difficult because of his massive and expansive popular appeal to the nation. It would have been much easier for the Republicans to run against Hillary Clinton than Barack, because Hillary did not have that great dynamic energy and appeal that Barack had. Even the Republican Party admitted that it was much easier to predict Hillary Clinton's campaign strategy than Barack's; however, Barack gave the Republican Party a nightmare with his explosive political and social energy that could publicly motivate, inspire, and surge at any given time in the campaign. It was very difficult for the Republican machine to plan against Barack's campaign because of the unpredictability that his dynamics and energy created.

The issue of race was definitely a factor in this historic election. Even though no one in the Republican Party would publicly admit to this, there was a silent hope that everyone in the Republican Party, and some Democrats, would have a resistance to voting for an Afro-American for president. This silent voice in the Republican Party was hoping, and this was its only chance of beating Barack. That is, that white America and non-black minorities would not vote for a black man for president. This silent hope that racism in America would stop an Obama presidency was that dark side of the Republican Party that did not work and has shone a bad racial image on the Republican Party.

Because Barack Obama, unlike Hillary Clinton, opposed the Iraq war and the Republican platform supported the war more initially and even more as the war progressed, this made it even harder for the Republican Party to keep Barack Obama out of the White House. First, there were many Republican voters, actually the majority of Republicans, felt the war was a mistake and not worth the fight as the 2007 and 2008 presidential campaigns actively started. Even though most of these Republicans agreed on Barack's position on the war, they did not mean that they would cross political party lines and vote for Barack. But the Republican Party did fear that 5 percent to 10 percent would vote for Barack if they felt that the Republican presidential candidate, Senator John McCain, was not going to start ending this war if he was elected president. This risk of losing Republican voters to Barack Obama was a high risk that John McCain hoped would not cost the Republican Party the race.

The majority of Americans, both Democrats and Republicans, were frustrated and pessimistic about the failing economy, the decreasing housing market, skyrocketing health-care prices, and many other issues that were negatively affecting the public. This attracted more supporters to Barack Obama. The public's political and economic frustration with the political system totally worked against the Republican Party, because it was a Republican administration that had ruled for the last seven years. The public has blamed the Republican Party for the failed policies, nationally and internationally, of the last seven years. The political party in power was blamed whether the blame was perception, reality, justified, or unjustified. This blame from the public was flamed by Barack's rhetoric that he was the personification of change to all these political, social, and economic problems. It was very difficult for the Republican Party to argue to the American public that they were the party of change and that Barack was not the candidate of change. This argument of which presidential candidate most represented change and could bring about the most change was an argument that the Republican Party lost and that Barack convincing won.

—Chapter 15—

Did You Believe Obama Was Going to Win?

(Obama's victory was based on the public believing he could win)

The Democratic primary elections and the presidential election were based on the American public's belief that Barack Obama could become the first Afro-American president of the United States. You are only as good as you believe you are, and if you believe, you can achieve anything. Jesus Christ said that if you believe, you can move mountains. Great athletes, such Michael Jordan, Muhammad Ali, and many great Olympic athletes, have spoken of and shown how one must first believe before one can act. The belief evolves into the action. The action is a result of the belief; this oneness of belief and action was what this nation and the world witnessed on election night, when the country believed in and voted in a young black president who was initially not expected to win. A positive belief creates a positive action, and a negative belief creates a negative action. On election night, this national and international belief was manifested as a political and social phenomenon, Barack Obama, the new president of the United States. When people simultaneously believe nationally and internationally, this global unification of believing in one purpose becomes a massive belief, and such a powerful global belief can drastically transform the entire political and social consciousness of this nation and world.

Why were believing and changing negative racial beliefs to positive racial beliefs relevant to Barack Obama becoming the Democratic nominee and finally our president. The belief that a black person could become president was the greatest factor that influenced the election of Barack, more influential than any campaign strategy or campaign ad. First, it was important that Barack Obama believed that he could become president and more important, strongly and optimistically believe that despite being Afro-American, he still could be president. If there had already been an Afro-American president, believing that a black person could be president would not have been difficult. However, given the ugly and dark racial history of this country, electing Barack Obama would require that this nation break through old racial and stereotypical beliefs that have prevented blacks from fairly advancing in this nation's political system. The negative and discriminatory belief that a black man could not be president had to be broken, and a positive belief had to be historically created and programmed into the belief system of American citizens.

Barack Obama and his campaign had to believe that he could be president. After his many impressive primary election wins against Hillary Clinton and receiving the Democratic nomination, he and his campaign had finally created and grounded the national belief that he could be the next president. They then had to do the most difficult thing: transfer this newly created positive and optimistic belief to the minds, emotions, hearts, and souls of American citizens. American citizens who never had or even seriously thought about having a black president. An American public, blacks and whites, many of whom never thought they would see a black president in their lifetime. However, this was also an America that was starting to experience one of the worst financial crises since the Great Depression and that had become desperate, frustrated, and open to change, new leadership, and a new way of political thinking and governing.

Our belief systems can be very tricky and deceptive, because we have conscious beliefs of which we are aware and subconscious and unconscious beliefs that we are unaware that they control what we think, believe, and create. The subconscious and unconscious beliefs are the ones that are so self-deceiving and, if negative, can be very destructive to the progress of an individual and even a nation. For example, there were probably Obama supporters who consciously believed in and wanted Obama to be president but who subconsciously and unconsciously did not believe that an Afro-American could or would ever be president. These debilitating racial beliefs negatively influenced the way white liberal Americans viewed Barack's chances of winning the presidency. Understand the massive task that Barack and his campaign had to do to eliminate these negative beliefs. They had to not only try to convince racist whites and those Americans who did not trust a black man governing the country but had to convince blacks and Barack's white supporters that he could win. Remember, for almost one year during the primary elections in 2007, Hillary Clinton, by a substantial margin, was leading Barack with the black vote until he won the Iowa caucus. This was the first big win for Barack, and it convinced most blacks that there was a greater possibility of there being the first Afro-American president. This was the beginning of the grounding of the confidence and belief that a Barack Obama presidency was possible. This national racist and discriminatory tradition and old belief of never electing a black president was so grounded that many Americans, even many blacks, accepted the reality of there never being a black president. This pessimistic belief that only a white person could be president in this highly diverse nation became a political and social tradition. Approximately 80 percent of blacks in this country were supporting Barack when he received the Democratic nomination, and many blacks still did not believe that his nomination would lead to an Obama presidency. Some thought, and seriously felt, that possibly Barack would be assassinated or that he would lose against Senator John McCain in the general election. A black man winning the presidency was still too difficult for many Americans, of all races, to believe. Could history and the new political dynamics create such a change in American politics? There were many Americans of different races who shared this lack of confidence and this pessimistic belief on a conscious, subconscious, or unconscious level. Barack Obama and his campaign were continuously aware of these negative unconscious beliefs that many Americans harbored deep within themselves. They enthusiastically continued to destroy the negative racial beliefs and ground these positive beliefs by continuing to win more primary elections and more delegates and superdelegates than Hillary Clinton. When he won the Democratic nomination, that totally destroyed the national belief that a black man could not be nominated by a major political party and run in the general presidential election. The reality of the first Afro-American president started to ground, and the impossible and unthinkable began to fade away like the setting sun. A few weeks before the presidential election in November 2008, the polls showed Barack with a solid lead in many crucial battleground states, and as a result of these great national poll numbers, the majority of Americans, even many Republicans, conceded and accepted that Barack would win. On November 4, 2008, Barack change a belief of racist thorns into a flower of opportunity, and the grounding of Martin Luther King Jr.'s dream was fully manifested in our great democratic political system. King's beautiful dream of each person judged by his or her character and abilities and not by his or her skin color had become a political and social reality.

This negative belief that a black person could not and should not be president in this democratic nation had sprouted out of the soil of bitter hate and fear hundreds of years before the 2008 presidential campaign. These severely damaging racial beliefs were created during and from our nation's dark, nasty, and embarrassing racial history. Blacks were slaves of white people and were forcefully taught and brainwashed for hundreds of years that they were inferior and had little self-worth. White America treated blacks like second-class citizens, and this viciously racial discrimination continued many years after blacks were freed from slavery. White America thought and said these negative and racially humiliating and inferiorizing beliefs, and black America heard and consciously and unconsciously programmed these hurtful and destructive beliefs deep into their minds, emotions, and souls. White people programmed into their minds and black people's minds the belief that white people were unconditionally superior to blacks. Unfortunately, the belief of racial discrimination is consciously and unconsciously floating around our country today. A belief that Barack Obama was finally able to transcend and be elected president and inspire and motivate the majority of Americans to transcend racially to that higher level of racial acceptance, racial tolerance, and racial love, which is part of the love for the human race.

First, it was essential that black people believe in themselves and reprogram these inferiorizing racial beliefs into positive and self-confident beliefs that finally created and grounded the first Afro-American president. Black America had to transcend the beliefs of self-inferiority, and this racial transcending was a racial healing for the black community. Barack's election as president destroyed many of those discriminatory beliefs that have been ingrained into this nation's psyche for many years. This transformation from not self-believing into self-believing had to be done before blacks could confidently cast their individual votes and help elect Barack. On election night, this positive belief grounded and was celebrated in the black community, and blacks across the country experienced an inner feeling of historic accomplishment, national fairness, and equal opportunity that had escaped them for many years. When Barack was elected, black America released hundreds of years of anger and resentment toward white America because of the vicious racism that white people had directed toward them. The Barack presidency was a silent forgiveness and silent pardon from black America to white America, a racial pardon and racial forgiveness that will benefit both and all races and allow this nation to rapidly move toward a racial love and a racial peace toward all human beings.

There are many positive ways that a Barack presidency has already and will affect the black community. For example, a national poll showed that after Barack was elected, 60 percent of black kids and 40 percent of white kids believed that they could become president. This drastic changing of black people's beliefs in themselves and the belief that they could achieve pure equality with white people and other races was fully realized when he was elected. Barack winning the top political position in the nation and world was, and is, a great example for all blacks and the beginning of pure equality for black America. Pure equality is when a person is given the same opportunity to achieve the same thing as another person or race. Barack competing on equal grounds with Hillary Clinton, winning the Democratic nomination, and finally winning the presidency by defeating Senator John McCain is an example of pure equality. The election of Barack Obama to the highest national office may be the greatest example of a black person and black America achieving pure equality with white America. This was the equal opportunity that blacks had dreamed about for hundreds of years. It is valuably essential that the black community learn and teach themselves to believe that great things can happen to them. This optimistic belief can transcend the black community to a higher economic, political, and social level.

The white Americans who supported Barack Obama also had to examine their own pessimistic political and social beliefs. They, like black people, had to learn to believe that Barack could win the presidency and that it was necessary to transcend these suppressed and unconscious negative racial beliefs that has programmed this country for many years to never elect a black president. These white supporters reprogrammed their unconscious and pessimistic racial beliefs into positive racial beliefs that consciously manifested itself on Election Day. They had to believe and see Barack not only as a presidential candidate but as the president.

If the American voters did not support Barack Obama because of his policies, politics, or personality, that would not be racism or discrimination but a free expression of the American citizens' personal and political opinion. That is appropriate and part of our great democratic process and our precious constitutional right to freedom of speech. However, American citizens who did not support and vote for Barack because he was black should humbly examine and look into their minds, hearts, and souls and throw out all racial hatred and prejudice. Even though a person does have a right, protected by free speech, to hate in this country, we, as a nation and individuals, must understand and be aware of how racial hate and all hate for our fellow human beings is so detrimental to creating a harmonious and prosperous nation. A prosperous nation whose social advancement and social success is dependent on all races living at an outer and inner peace with each other. American citizens who did not vote for Barack should make sure that their vote against him was based on his political character and his ability to govern the country, not based on the color of his skin. These American citizens should toss these racist beliefs into the ocean of "no more discrimination" so that these beliefs can be eternally dissolved at the bottom of the ocean of racial justice and fairness and float back to the top as pure racial equality and racial love. It is essential that this nation get past racism and embrace this positive belief that all people should have the equal opportunity to achieve and succeed in this magnificent nation that we and the world know as the United States of America.

The last barrier that Barack had to overcome before getting the Democratic nomination was to convince the superdelegates of the Democratic Party that they should nominate him to run in the November election. This could only be done when the belief that he could win was grounded by the American public and the news media. The American public finally believed that Barack should be the Democratic nominee by voting for him in the Democratic primary elections, while the news media daily showed this young presidential candidate doing well in the televised debates and the polls. They had to believe in Barack before pledging their votes for him, and their confidence in him increased as he started solidly leading Hillary Clinton in the polls. Most of the superdelegates became convinced that Barack Obama would be a stronger and better Democratic nominee than Hillary after he won more primary elections, had more total delegates, and a higher popular vote. These factors greatly influenced the superdelegates' decision to nominate him as the Democratic Party's nominee. The superdelegates' belief in Barack fed off the public's belief in his ability to win the presidency. The more the public believed in Barack, the more the superdelegates believed in Barack. It was important for Barack to continue to win primary after primary so he could further convince the public and the superdelegates that it was realistic and pragmatic for a black man to be the next president of the United States.

A belief system, whether negative or positive, is like a seed that is planted, grows, and becomes a large tree. The belief in an Obama presidency was politically and socially planted in the American public when he announced his candidacy in January 2007. Since then, the American public has amazingly and impressively watched this seed of faith and self-belief grow into a tree of political, social, and historic achievement. The American public saw this seed of self-confidence and hope sprout out of the political ground and start slowly growing when Hillary Clinton was leading Barack in the polls by a margin of 20 percent to 30 percent early in the primary elections. At that time, the majority of blacks were not supporting Barack. Since then, this seed of believing that an Afro-American could be president has grown into a flower of political hope, political dynamics, political confidence, and finally, the historic reality: Barack Obama, the forty-fourth president of the United States. The seeds of opportunity and destiny broke through the political soil and grew into the positive reality that was an inspirational, highly intelligent, black man governing this great nation. This seed, the Obama political phenomenon, which was planted across our nation in the minds of American citizens, is now a beautiful tree that has shown no sign of not continuing to grow and bloom to its fullest potential in our political system. From January 2007, the official beginning of Barack Obama's campaign, to Election Day, November 4, 2008, this belief nationally and internationally manifested itself into a global reality.

This transcending positive belief of having a black president was challenged and rejected in the minds of some Americans because of their racial prejudices and fears; however, it was freely accepted in the minds of millions upon millions of Americans who were open to political and social enlightenment and who desired change and advancement to a higher political and social level in this country. Barack continued to water the positive beliefs about him with the fertilizer of hope, confidence, and optimism, and he did not reject or show disdain for the Americans who racially disliked him. He always stayed above racial division and racial hatred with the hope that one day, all racist Americans would mentally and emotionally cross over to that higher level of racial enlightenment. This racial enlightenment is a level where racial ignorance, racial narrow-mindedness, and racial hatred cannot exist. Some Americans, who were slightly fearful of voting for a black man for president, mentally and emotionally crossed over to support Barack when the economy started to collapse approximately a month before the election. These racially sensitive white Americans decided to put their economic security ahead of their racial fears and decided to vote for Barack Obama. It is arguable whether Barack Obama would have become the forty-fourth president had the economy not become so unstable and the American public not become so pessimistic about the economy. This positive racial crossover from white America to support an Afro-American candidate gradually began to happen before his Democratic nomination, continued after his nomination, occurred on Election Day, and will continue during his four, possibly eight years. White America helped elect a president who will lead a nation that will always rise like the morning sun and will one day racially bloom to a level where unconditional love for the human race overrides racial hate and prejudice toward our fellow American citizens.

The tipping point for the majority of Americans to believe that Barack would and should be the Democratic nominee and possibly president was after he won the Potomac primaries that consisted of Maryland, Virginia, and Washington, D.C. At that point in the campaign, Barack had won eight consecutive states against Hillary Clinton. This string of victories created a new type of momentum that created an energy, enthusiasm, and confidence to continue winning, but more important, it grounded a new political and social belief that this young, dynamic Afro-American was the chosen one to be nominated and possibly elected president of the United States.

This grounded optimistic belief not only created an Obama presidency but it has already started creating many changes that Barack had articulated around the country during his campaign, such as building capitalism from the bottom to top instead of solely from the top to the bottom. He has already proposed to create jobs directly for poor and middle-class citizens, not just depend on corporations and the wealthy to trigger money down to the middle class and poor. Barack Obama is the personification of we Americans believing in and loving ourselves as a great nation. He is a personification of the transcending of negative racial beliefs and national unification around a common purpose. A change that can only be done when old beliefs have been eliminated and new beliefs of hope, confidence, and faith have been created. This higher level of political and social beliefs is the beginning of an era in which a person of any skin color can have the opportunity to lead this great nation and set a standard and belief in oneself so high that no negative belief can ever hold this nation in mental, political, or social bondage again.

—Chapter 16—
The Jealousy Factor

(Barack's greatest obstacle)

Whether it was political or personal, jealousy was one of the most negative energies for Barack to overcome and transform into a positive and winning energy during the 2008 presidential elections. Jealousy was directed toward Barack, will continue to be directed at him, and will escalate after he is elected. This political and social jealousy of Barack Obama came from people of different races, social and political status, and positions. Jealousy can be a great barrier to anyone's success; however, it can be overcome and transcended with personal strength, courage, perseverance, and a highly intelligent understanding of people. Barack Obama showed that he had all these characteristics and also the self-confidence, self-respect, self-love, and self- and political discipline to overcome the jealousy that was targeted at him.

Barack Obama had many dynamic attributes that caused some people, both leaders and the public, to be very jealous of him. The first attribute was his gifted ability to envision, motivate, and inspire people and the nation. Many leaders and his fellow politicians were very jealous of this amazing attribute, because they wished that they had this natural gift of being a visionary and transformational figure. Barack understood that there was and will be more jealousy directed at him; however, he was intelligent and wise enough not to trust jealous people, watch them from every corner of his eyes, and rose above this negativity and silly jealousy. Those who were envious of him will always be looking for any opportunity to undermine and to destroy him politically.

As I wrote this chapter, there was a part of me that did not want to write this chapter at all. I wish that I could skip it; however, it is necessary to discuss how jealousy, as vicious as it is, always rides alongside political greatness and political success. With all the positive things that Barack Obama brought into the political arena, he also triggered a strong political jealousy throughout the country. This jealousy existed from the leaders to American citizens. It was important that this chapter be written, because many people created many reasons why they did not support Barack Obama. Many of the reasons sounded rational and legitimate; however, the underlining and unconscious reasons for many people not supporting Barack Obama was jealousy of his quick rise to power in American politics.

The big question for Barack during his campaign was whether he had enough support and momentum to outweigh the negative and detrimental energy of jealousy from those who disliked him. He did have enough support and positive energy to lift him through the negative realms of jealousy, because if he did not, he would not be politically where he is today. After overcoming these political jealousy barriers that tried to stop his political momentum, Barack continued to increase and use his high energy, high-moving dynamics, and the higher political consciousness and awareness that had allowed him to transcend and stay above any jealousy that he could politically or personally hurt him.

There were voters who were not voting for Barack because of personal and political jealousy of him. Barack was the perfect example of the fulfillment of the American dream, and many individuals in the country looked at Barack with total envy, because they wanted to achieve the American dream for their lives. Just as there were millions who were inspired and motivated by Barack's political success, many were jealous that this young politician had achieved such quick political success. Instead of those jealous Americans viewing Barack as a success story, they viewed him as someone to be envied silently; some even directly allowed their jealousy to speak loudly. This jealousy of Barack coming from the American voters was not just from white voters; it was from the blacks and other races as well. Barack was aware that this jealousy was out there and knew that this was a negative reality that he accepted.

Jealousy from Black Leaders

At the beginning of Barack's campaign in early 2007, and until the South Carolina primary in 2008, Barack struggled to get the support of black people. Hillary Clinton, for almost a year, convincingly led him in the Afro-American vote. I was not sure if the blacks did not support Barack, because he was biracial Afro-American. I almost concluded that there was a racial jealousy directed at Barack from blacks across the country, but that proved not to be true. After the South Carolina primary, Barack had the majority of blacks on his side, and their support for him seemed solidified.

However, during the primary elections, there were a few blacks, mainly some black leaders, who made up that 20 percent or less who did not support Barack. They were jealous of how easily Barack had climbed the political ladder and was headed toward being the next U.S. president. These black citizens and black leaders had allowed their jealousy to blind them from Barack's greatness and put them on the wrong side of history if Barack won the presidency. Even though these black leaders argued that they supported Hillary Clinton because of her experience and strength, there was a sense, of course arguably, that the root of their support for Hillary and lack of support for Barack was jealousy. After all, imagine those black leaders who have been in politics for years and wanted to and dreamed of being president, and out of nowhere, Barack appears and is now on the verge of holding the highest position in the nation and world.

Jealousy from other minorities is a form of racial jealousy that Barack has and will continue to face. Even though Barack constantly makes progress in winning over other minorities, there are probably those individual minorities that harbor a deep jealousy of Barack, because he is not of their minority's race. It is the desire of any minority to have a person from their race run for president of the United States, but to have a person from another race run for president could create a racial jealousy toward the presidential candidate and his race. A jealousy that will hopefully be destroyed by open-mindedness, understanding, fairness, justice, racial tolerance, love, and unification. However, it seems that as time moves along, Barack is starting to turn the jealousy that minorities have of him into love for him as a great, inspiring leader of all American people.

One of the biggest jealousies confronting Barack is the jealousy of him making great and monumental history in the country. Everybody instinctively wants to be part of history or to be history themselves. Barack's chance to be the first Afro-American elected president is sparking much jealous, but there is even more jealousy than that. John F. Kennedy's daughter said of Barack Obama that he is the most inspiring leader that she has seen since her father. Other people have said that Barack Obama is the most inspiring leader that they have seen in the last fifty years. Even though many people are excited about this kind of aspiration and inspiration of a leader, there are some jealous people, and there will always be, who will hate to see great history created by a great person like Barack Obama.

Another big obstacle that Barack must overcome is the jealousy that some superdelegates may have of him. The big question is whether the jealousy is great enough to prevent enough superdelegates from giving him the Democratic nomination. Another question is will the superdelegates put aside any jealousy that they may have of Barack Obama's success and do what is fair, right, and best for the Democratic Party.

Why would a superdelegate be personally or politically jealous of Barack? There are many reasons. First, superdelegates, who are big insiders that consist of present and former elected officials, may be jealous that they never became president or did not have as much quick political success as Barack Obama. Second, many of the superdelegates may envy Barack because of such a youthful political career. They may grudgingly feel that Barack, who was only a U.S. senator for one and half years, has not paid his dues as a leader and politician in Washington. However, the uncommitted superdelegates may override any jealousy that they may have for Barack by voting their conscience, a conscience that is fully aware that Barack will not only be a great president who will transform the Democratic Party, but he will be a great asset to and ambassador for the Democratic Party for the next twenty to thirty years.

Barack's positive attitude keeps him above all jealousy and is the main reason that he has become victim to others' jealousy and enviousness of him. This positive attitude is the cure to defeating and winning over jealousy, because as this positive political and social energy spreads across the country and world, it is very difficult for jealousy to function in optimism and faith. It very hard for jealousy to continue to fight against confidence, determination, courage, and perseverance. These are all qualities that Barack has and will need to withstand the vicious attacks of jealousy that will be hurdled at him during this election and in the White House.

Will these personal and political jealousies stop Barack from getting the Democratic nomination and winning the White House? Probably not. Nothing seems to be able to stop the Obamentum yet, and he seems to have overcome all political hurdles and obstacles to this point. Barack knows that no matter how great jealousy is, it can be overcome with a grounded consciousness of hope and political love for your nation and your participation in your nation's political system. As more people start to participate in our nation's politics, the need to be jealous of Barack's political success will be replaced by one's love to be part of the beginning of great history and great changes in our nation.

—Chapter 17—
Transcending Liberalism and Conservatism

(The beginning of the age of political enlightenment)

Barack Obama Could Become One of the Greatest Presidents Ever

As the country enjoyed this electrifying politician and leader, Barack Obama, there was very little calm from so much excitement for anyone to stop, think, and imagine what kind of president he would be. Barack had shown a high political level, high political intellect, an inspiring and dynamic leadership, and the potential to become one of the greatest presidents ever. During the campaign, Barack's political opponents, such as Senator Hillary Clinton and Senator John McCain, criticized him for his lack of political experience, and while he argued that he had the judgment and pragmatic intellect to be a good president, very few people, even Barack's strongest supporters, had not seriously thought what kind of president he should be. Many of these Barack supporters had publicly stated that they did not specifically know what kind of president Barack would be. We had heard Barack's supporters speak that he is the president of change and has great political and social visions for our nation. What will the change be like, and what kind of new politics and new government will Barack's social vision bring? We heard some of Barack's positions on health care, the fairness of tax cuts, how to fix an ailing economy, and resolve the Afghanistan and the Iraq wars, but what will a leader of such high energy and political dynamics do for the country, the people, the nation's image, and the many problems facing our nation? Will he use his dynamics to govern from the center as a moderate leader, be extremely to the left, or be moderately conservative in some things? Will he combine both conservatism and liberalism to unite people of both parties, or will he just politically and socially transcend conservatism and liberalism as we know it? Will he create a politics and a way of governing that is equivalent to his high energy, political intellect, and high political consciousness and awareness? Has Barack been holding back the method and style that he will use to govern this great nation when he is inaugurated on January 20, 2009? Was he just trying to get through politically and win a hard-fought campaign and then surprise and show this nation and the world how great of a president and leader he can be? Is he going to shock the Democratic Party just as much as the Republican Party with his new style of governing and running this great nation? Will Barack be the Michael Jordan of politics? Michael Jordan was a very good college basketball player, but when he entered the NBA, no one ever dreamed that he would excel to such a high level of pro basketball, arguably the highest level ever. Barack may excel to a level of government and politics that we have never imagined or seen.

Transcending Liberalism and Conservatism

There was always a sense that once Barack won the presidency he would bring a political level to Washington, D.C that would transcend the beliefs of liberalism and conservatism. A political level that would transcend both Republican and Democratic ideas and allow both Democrats and Republicans to function in harmony. A high political level that allows liberals and conservatives to be tolerant of each other's beliefs and to unite under a common message of creating a better government and a more politically and socially advanced nation. Barack Obama, as president, will cause the creation of a new Democratic Party and a new Republican Party that will care more about solutions to problems than whether the problem or issue is solved from a conservative or liberal point of view.

Barack has the political level to transcend conservatism and liberalism, because he uses rational thinking to create rational solutions and a belief system that creates better ways of governing in this country. A political and social belief system that enables every American citizen to believe in him- or herself and to believe that a better life is possible in this country. A belief system that will encourage each American citizen to create big dreams and visions and have the confidence to make these visions a reality. A belief system that leads the hearts, minds, and souls of every American citizen to set the highest standard of total living and total prosperity for life. During a Barack presidency, his ability to have big visions for the country will become publicly contagious and rub off on the American public, and the American public, both conservatives and liberals, will have big visions and big dreams for the nation and themselves. Both the Republican and the Democratic parties will be the political parties of big dreams and great political and social visions. With great visions and dreams come big solutions. Big solutions to problems and issues that will advance our nation to the level that we, American citizens, daily desire and are striving to attain.

The Age of Political Enlightenment

As president of the United States of America, Barack will lead this new age of political, social, and personal enlightenment. This political and social enlightenment will be embraced by both liberals and conservatives and will inspire American citizens to seek and create solutions to our national and global problems. With enlightenment comes faith, confidence, hope, intellectualism, pragmatism, creativity, a high level of understanding, a rational compassion, and the personal desire to be all that you should be. This political enlightenment will look beyond silly political party bickering and concentrate on solving problems by creating many practical and creative solutions. Creative political and social solutions will enhance our nation and create policies in which the American people can have faith and confidence and live better lives as American citizens. That is, better lives with more opportunities for this generation and many generations to come.

The political intellect of Barack is what this country has been in need of for many years. It is a level of politics that this country has never had. Barack has a political level that examines the mind-set and the reasons behind the creation of our nation's policies. A good example of this was in one televised presidential debate with Hillary Clinton. When asked about the Iraq war, Barack said that he does not want to just end the war, but he wants to change the mind-set that made us go to war in the first place. This high level of thinking will bring a new direction to America and create an era of new domestic and foreign policies. The Obama presidency will inspire and encourage American citizens to change the way they view their nation and the world. A view of the nation and world that will help us to prevent problems from happening before they happen, and when they do happen, we will be able to solve them with patience, pragmatic intellectualism, and with much sound-minded reasoning. This kind of sound-minded reasoning will be the sign that our nation has entered into the age of political enlightenment.

An Obama Presidency Will Inspire and Create a New Thinking and New Political and Social Behavior from American Citizens

Barack understands how one personally believes and thinks affects the way one's nation politically behaves, and this political behavior is what dictates whether our nation creates and has good or bad policies. Barack knows that to change the behavior of the country, the leaders of the country must change their political and social beliefs and mentality. This mental change of the leadership can only be done when the people unite and change their thinking, and this unification of a political message and political philosophy of the citizens will influence the political and social philosophy of the nation's leadership. The citizens' positive and powerful influence on our leaders will cause them to make foreign and domestic policies that are a reflection of sound-minded and rational political beliefs and political thinking. Sound-minded and rational political beliefs that will create a political system where both the citizens and the leaders can have the same vision and same mind-set about how this great superpower, the United States of America, should be governed. When a country reaches this political and social level in which the political beliefs of the people become the same as the political beliefs of the leaders, then this nation can become the kind of nation of which the forefathers dreamed. That is, a nation where enlightened people lead the leaders, and the leaders follow the great national vision of the people. Barack has the political intellect to inspire the American people to mentally rise to that level where they will be able to, with their political confidence, inspire the leaders to lead the country to a higher political level. This inspiration that the leaders receive from the public will be returned from the leader to the public, which will move the public to get involved and participate in our political system and government. This political participation will create a sense of political and national identity, love, pride, and inner happiness for our country and a deep appreciation to be an American citizen.

America Enters a New Era of Politics

Barack will help American citizens and our nation's leaders transcend political party differences, which will allow both Democrats and Republicans, leaders and citizens, to come together, rationally argue, debate issues, and unite with a vision for the country. A vision that will create policies and laws that will make this great nation a greater nation.

Barack's ability to get the nation to transcend unnecessary bickering over issues and unite under one common solution for each of the nation's major problems will be the basis of him becoming a great president and this nation becoming a greater and more politically and socially advanced nation. The ability of a nation to transcend its differences in order to improve and make it a better place to live is the beginning of the new era of politics that Barack Obama spoke of during his campaign. The dynamics of the nation coming together is a high-level national experience that has only been felt during certain times in our nation's history. In a time of crisis, people usually unite nationally and pull together; however, it should not take a national catastrophe for the nation to unite to achieve a national and common purpose. An example of the last time this nation united was on September 11, 2001, when we were attacked by bin Laden and his terrorist followers. The American citizens' unification quickly healed the country and put our nation back on its feet, and we were able to move on with our lives. In the days following 9-11, Congress, Democrats and Republicans, unified to help defend the nation and do what they thought was best for the country after such a tragedy. This kind of unification can be done by our leaders, Congress, and the public in everyday politics. However, there must be a strong desire and a grounded consciousness and awareness of the importance of political resolve and moving the country forward and in a direction that is good for our nation and the world. Barack's leadership will keep our country reaching for the highest political sun and the shiniest political star. When this happens, our nation will glow with an overflow of political and social enlightenment.

A New Political Enthusiasm

This national political enlightenment that Barack Obama will bring into the White House will shine and spread through this nation and to the world. This new enlightenment will shine from the top to the bottom and from the bottom to the top. That is, it will flow from the rich to the poor, the poor to the rich, the leaders to the American citizens, and the American citizens to its leaders. The Barack presidency will not only be a phenomenon in this country but also worldwide and will show how to govern a nation to a level that this country and other nations have not seen. This is a new way of governing, allowing one's enlightened political intellect to guide the nation and American citizens to a level and form of government based on much political and social wisdom, vision, and a high public enthusiasm.

Enthusiasm helps people to overcome political barriers and mental and emotional barriers. The high energy that Barack possesses is just what the doctor ordered for this nation and the world. This high energy consists of much enthusiasm, hope, self-confidence, love for oneself and nation, inspiration, aspiration, motivation, and the faith that the political vision for the country will be created and all citizens will benefit from the many prosperous opportunities. This new enthusiasm creates a dynamics and the will to be better American citizens and better people.

Can Barack help this nation transcend to a level that will set a great example and the highest standard for other nations? Will Barack Obama set the United States on a high trophy shelf so that it will be the perfect model of how a nation should be governed, and will he demonstrate the highest and most rational form of democracy? Will other nations look to Barack to lead the world as he leads our nation, and will he become a global political sensation, bring us closer to other countries, and make our enemies our friends? We, American citizens and the world, are waiting for the grounding of this highly anticipated political level. When Barack was elected and inaugurated as president of the United States in 2009, everyone will wait for this change to happen. History will loudly speak that the time has come for the nation to accept what the new history has to offer to our nation, which is in need of drastic political change from an old history. An old history that has become stagnated with political and social resistance to change and a great fear of a brighter future that will create a better tomorrow for us, the American public.

Wade Lewis (The Magic Man)
Photograph by Jeff Davis